CRYSTAL
GRID
ORACLE

DELUXE EDITION

Written and illustrated by
NICOLA McINTOSH

CRYSTAL
GRID
ORACLE

DELUXE EDITION

ROCKPOOL

A Rockpool book
PO Box 252
Summer Hill
NSW 2130
Australia

rockpoolpublishing.com
Follow us! **f** 〇 rockpoolpublishing
Tag your images with #rockpoolpublishing

First published in 2018 as *Crystal Grid Oracle*
(ISBN 9781925682601) by Rockpool Publishing.

This deluxe edition published in 2023 by Rockpool Publishing
includes 36 new cards.

ISBN: 9781922785145

Design and typesetting by Daniel Poole, Rockpool Publishing
Edited by Lisa Macken

Printed and bound in China
10 9 8 7 6 5 4 3 2 1

CONTENTS

INTRODUCTION

Following the success of the *Crystal Grid Oracle*, this deluxe edition has the inclusion of a second deck of 36 new crystal grid cards, making it an oracle of 72 cards.

This deluxe oracle is a tool to aid spiritual growth and provides the next step in expanding your awareness of yourself with help from the crystal kingdom. As a new age is heralded in you need to shift what guides you, as old patterns and behaviours that once served you no longer will. The deck asks you to expand your thinking, seeing and perceiving by pushing yourself one step further. Completely trust yourself and spirit and realise that the oracle is much more than just a tool: it is a direct link to spirit and source. Let go of your fears and trust the information you receive. Most importantly, take time out of your busy schedule, grab a cuppa and connect with the incredible energy that works through this deck. If you make this a regular practice of self-care this oracle will become a tool for your spiritual and evolutionary growth.

Each of the 72 cards also has an exercise for you to practise that will expand your understanding of what the card is asking of you.

Nature is a gift to learn from: every creature, plant, rock or crystal has something to teach you. You can learn by what nature might reflect in you: the colour, shape and arrangement may all have some significance to you because your external environment is merely a reflection of your internal environment. When you begin to observe how your external environment behaves around you, you can understand what you are projecting into the world. This allows you to see inside your being for true healing and growth.

By connecting with nature you are connecting with the all that is, with source. When you do this you will find a connection to your true self and will ultimately find peace. Each crystal has a particular resonance or vibration that makes it unique to that stone and therefore has a specific purpose. Also, every crystal has a spirit or particular consciousness that can work through it. You can call upon the spirit of the stone to aid or teach you what the gift of that particular stone has to offer you, and it may also have insight unique to you.

You don't have to have the physical stone in your possession in order to work with it, which is what makes working with this oracle so special. *You can still work with the energy of each crystal in this deck even if you don't have the physical crystal with you*. If you do want to purchase crystals I suggest you start with quartz, the most abundant mineral on earth and easily accessible. Also, you can use it to substitute any other crystal in the deck. We can call any crystal energy to us with the use of quartz because it is an amplifier of energy; in fact, we don't need any crystals at all to do this but quartz certainly helps.

A crystal grid is the bringing together of many crystals to create a unified, magnified energy with a specific intent. It is a physical manifestation of your intent, which is resonated out to the universe. You might like to learn more from my book *Crystal Grid Secrets*.

It is time to expand your consciousness to understand that the energy of crystals is available to you at any time, that all you need to do is call upon it. Crystals can teach us through their form and also through their energetic signature.

HOW TO USE
THE CARDS

One of the most important parts of reading oracle cards is how you interpret the imagery, colours and words. Each card has a crystal grid in which the centre crystal is the main focus of the meaning of the card. As crystals can have many meanings, I have included three keywords for each card you can refer to. This guidebook gives you my interpretation of the energy coming through the cards and information about the crystals, but when you work with them over time you may feel other meanings come through that are relevant to you and your work. Always trust what you sense even if you think it's silly, because the more you trust the more you will be able to decipher the images.

Shuffle the deck and call in the crystal spirits to be with you. I normally say: 'Crystal spirits, please be with me now. I ask for your guidance.' Working with spirit is a relationship composed of respect, honesty and trust. Always ask permission and always thank the energies that work through the cards for you, because the more you make this connection the more you will receive from your oracle.

One thing I also feel is important to state here is that the cards are used as triggers to bring through your guidance and the energy that has chosen to work through this oracle. Look at the oracle as a means to communicate with this energy and for it to communicate with you, and over time the cards will resonate with a mix of beautiful energies. Don't be limited to the description in this guidebook as to what the cards are for. Think of the guidebook as just that, a guide, and don't let it restrict you in any way.

There is no right or wrong way to pick out your cards: just pull them out of the deck any way you like and go where you are drawn to go. If any fall out, keep them aside as they always have meaning in your reading and provide a little extra information spirit is trying to communicate to you. If I am reading for others I allow them to shuffle the deck and pick their own cards, but you can also do the same for them. When you trust that the right information will come through no matter what, you let go of the fear that something can be done incorrectly.

As with the original *Crystal Grid Oracle* there are no hard and fast rules when it comes to using this oracle. Here are several quick and simple readings for when you are a little time poor:

- Pull one card a day to give you guidance on what to expect or what energy to be aware of for the day.

- Pull one card to meditate with.

- Pull a three-card spread, which may represent the past, present and future.

You can do a reading for a person without them saying anything about what they are there for, but I find it always flows better and opens up an incredibly powerful reading when they are open and can tell you how the cards relate to their situation.

Be guided by other markers you might come across with the cards: the colours, crystal arrangements, symbols or imagery that may come to you. Do the crystals have other meanings to you? Spirit may send through clues or messages for specific cards that resonate with you, so be confident in trusting your intuition. The more you use the oracle the more familiar and confident you will become with each of the cards. Remember that this is the deluxe edition, so there are no limits!

For more in-depth readings you may like to work with the following spreads, which I find incredibly powerful.

OBSTACLE SPREAD

Draw four cards and lay them out as shown below. I like to tell spirit what the cards will represent before I pick each one, as I feel this communicates to them clearly what I need to know before being guided to select the card:

- ♦ **Card 1** represents where you are now.
- ♦ **Card 2** represents where you want to be or where you will be in 12 months' time.
- ♦ **Card 3** represents the steps needed to get where you want to be.
- ♦ **Card 4** represents the obstacles you might need to overcome to get there.

LIFE PATH SPREAD

I use the life path spread when I do readings for others or I want to do something more in-depth for myself. I find it works so well for people who want guidance on a specific issue or as a general reading when they are not sure what they want to know about.

When using the cards in larger spreads it's important to see how they relate to one another. Draw seven cards, or if you are reading for someone else have them pick seven cards, then lay each one face down on top of one other. If any fall out or the other person picks too many, keep them aside for the end. Lay them out in the sequence below, starting with the first card they placed down:

- ♦ **Card 1:** you and your strength.
- ♦ **Card 2:** your life.
- ♦ **Card 3:** what helps bring happiness to your life.
- ♦ **Card 4:** obstacles you need to overcome.
- ♦ **Card 5:** a message from your angels.
- ♦ **Card 6:** a message from your guides.
- ♦ **Card 7:** a message from your heart.
- ♦ **Extra card/s:** these are usually extra messages you need to know or they back up what has come through.

These indicate the meanings of the cards, which is a great place to start. If you're using this spread to look into a specific issue, I sometimes find that the cards on the left represent more of the issue, which will become apparent as you move from card to card. You might then start to recognise how certain cards relate back to other cards in the spread or a theme will reveal itself through the reading.

EXERCISES

For each card in the deck there is an exercise to help you look within for answers, but also to help push you one step further if you need more help. It is up to you to put in the work, although you should make sure it is a fun experience. If it feels like a chore you won't get true value from it. The exercises can be incredibly powerful and can propel you forward so fast it will open up a whole new way of working through the issues in your life.

MEDITATING VERSUS JOURNEYING

In many of the exercises I might suggest meditating or journeying. Shamanic journeying may be something new to you, so don't feel daunted by the thought of it. Anyone can journey: it is very much like a visual meditation and sometimes you might not be able to tell the difference. Don't put pressure on yourself to visualise anything, as it is something that comes with practice. Some people don't see anything but instead feel things. Your intention for the journey is the key.

To get started it's a great idea to write down what you want to visualise when you do your meditation or journey. I start by writing it out and then voice recording my notes into my phone so I can listen to it at any time. Make sure you read slowly in a monotone voice. It's good practice to turn your phone on to airplane mode to replay it, light some incense or a candle and set a space for yourself that makes the practice feel special and calming.

When I journey I don't observe myself doing things: I see everything as though I am doing it in person. For instance, if I visualise myself walking through a field, I don't picture it as though I am watching something on the television; I literally take my full consciousness with me. I look down and see my legs walking through the grass, the grass brushing against my legs, the sun on my face, the wind blowing my hair. When I touch a tree I see my hand reach out and feel the rough bark under my fingers and feel the energy exchange between the tree and myself.

You may feel as though you are making it up and to some extent you are, but you need to experience it to understand it. The more you practise the more you will learn from it. I gain the most knowledge when I write my experiences down, because when you put it into words it will make much more sense. It will be different for everyone and that's okay, because there are no rules. Just know that much insight can be gained from the practice of journeying, and once you start it will excite you to know what can be achieved.

Meditating is similar to journeying, although rather than travelling somewhere you focus your mind on a particular object, activity or thought in order to shift your attention to reach a state of calm and centredness. You can also do visualisation meditations, which are similar to journeying. Both meditating and journeying are intended to shift your consciousness into a different state, so start with what feels comfortable for you. There are many guided meditations on the internet to get you started, and more information on shamanic journeying can be found on my website: www.spiritstone.com.au.

Following are some examples of exercises that will get you started. Let them be a guide and add to them if you feel guided to do so.

TREE OF LIFE GROUNDING EXERCISE

I do this while standing to feel as much like a tree as possible. You may have your own way of doing it, so use whatever feels comfortable for you. The tree of life exercise is an extremely valuable part of any spiritual undertaking that creates your connection with the earth and to the energies above. You should draw your energy from it just as a tree draws its energy through its roots and leaves. To ground and connect:

- Stand comfortably with your feet shoulder width apart and unlock your knees. You can also do this lying down or sitting up in a seat if that is more comfortable for you. Find your centre and breathe out all your tension.

- If you are standing, rock back and forth on your feet a little to find a good position so that your balance becomes distributed evenly over your feet, and make sure your knees are unlocked. Let them bend a little. You will feel any areas of tension that you need to let go of.

- Close your eyes and take a few deep breaths to relax and focus. Picture roots growing out of your feet and tailbone and into the earth. Send the roots down through the earth and see them pushing through all the layers.

- Picture a big white ball of energy in the centre of the earth. Connect your roots to the ball of light and picture it moving up through your roots, like a tree drawing up water and nutrients from the soil. Draw the light up through the soles of your feet and tailbone. Draw the light up through your body to your heart. It may be easier to draw the energy up on every in breath to create a good rhythm.

- See the light go down to your fingertips and back to your heart. See the light go up through the centre of your head. See it extending out through branches sprouting from your head, shoulders and arms. Lift your arms to also draw the power up and to feel and become the tree. Send the energy out through the ends of the branches and out through the leaves into the sky. Watch it extend up through the layers of the atmosphere into space and reach up to touch the sun or moon (depending on the time of day) or perhaps a star.

- Feel the sun, moon or star light on your face as you draw down its white light through your head, and trace the way back that the earth light came through you: down through your head, to your heart, your fingertips and back to your heart, down through your body, out through your feet and through the roots. Connect with the ball of white light in the centre of the earth.

- Now that you have connected like the tree of life it is important to shield yourself. This will help deflect any negative energies but will also contain the energy you now have flowing through you. Picture a big white or gold bubble in front of you that you step into, or maybe a shield that pops up all around you. Go with whatever feels right for you. Fill your shield full of white light and know you are protected. Now you can proceed with an exercise or ritual.

SAMPLE CRYSTAL MEDITATION

For this meditation and shamanic journey you can use any crystal you like or crystal grid card from the deck; just insert its name where necessary. You might like to record it in your own words and play it back, being sure to speak slowly and giving yourself pauses and time to ask your questions. Keep your voice slow and monotonal.

Make sure you are comfortable and won't be disturbed. Place the crystal or card that you wish to connect with in front of you or hold it in your hand. Close your eyes, relax and slow your breathing. Picture the crystal or card in front of you in your mind's eye, and with every exhale you do breathe love to the crystal or card. On every inhale, draw love from the crystal or card in through your heart. Repeat the cycle of breathing in the love and exhaling the love until you feel a shift in your energy. Remain focused on your breathing and let any other thoughts come and go from your mind.

When you feel you are in a complete state of connection and relaxation you might like to ask the crystal or card for guidance and then listen with all your senses to receive what spirit has to tell you. It may be in words, images, feelings, smells or just a sense, as spirit communicates with us in many ways.

When you feel as though the session is drawing to an end, thank the crystal spirit for its guidance and give it your gratitude. Gently open your eyes and record what you experienced. Don't worry if you didn't get anything first try; it will come the more you practise.

SAMPLE CRYSTAL SHAMANIC JOURNEY

There are three worlds in shamanism: the upper, middle and lower worlds. Each world is visited depending on what kind of helper spirit you wish to meet:

- The lower world is generally for work with ancestors, shadow work and crystal and plant spirits and so on. Working with the lower and upper worlds first is suggested before moving on to the middle.

- The middle world is for working with the energies of our physical world such as unhealthy attachments and soul loss.

- The upper world is for accessing a higher spiritual plane such as the akashic records and spirit guides, and where we can go to get a higher perspective on things.

Shamanic journeying is usually started with the sound of a drum, which helps shift your consciousness to a different state. You can download drumming apps or music to your phone or use a physical drum.

For this journey you may like to meet a helper guide, crystal spirit or teacher of some sort. Sit in a comfortable position where you will not be disturbed. Do a grounding exercise such as the tree of life exercise above and then call in your spirit guides, helper spirits or animal totems. Close your eyes and feel yourself within your physical body. Feel the air on your skin and see in your mind's eye your totem animals ready and waiting to walk with you on your journey.

When you feel ready, in your mind's eye see yourself in a beautiful field with a massive oak tree before you. Look at the tree as though you are seeing out of your physical eyes and look down to see the long grass around your legs. Walk slowly towards the tree and feel the grass sweep past your legs. Feel the breeze on your face and your loose clothing flowing around you as you get closer and closer to the tree. When you get to the tree, see your hand reach out to touch the trunk and feel the texture of the bark under your fingers. Look up to the see beautiful oak leaves and acorns hanging from the branches.

Looking down, see the large gnarled roots and notice what seems to be a hole in the ground. Ask the mighty oak if you may enter and wait to get a sensation from the tree that it is okay. Go into the hole, and as you enter you will feel a shift in space in time. As your eyes adjust to the dark you will realise that the hole is getting larger and deeper and sloping downwards. Follow the track and notice you are spiralling downwards into the earth until you get to a doorway. Reach out to the handle and open the door and go through.

You will again sense a shift in your reality. Continue forward and downward, following the track, which is winding down and around until you come to another doorway. Open the door and walk through, again sensing the shift in reality. Continue walking the path, feeling yourself going deeper and deeper underground until you come across one last door. Open this door and step through. Once you step through your eyes will adjust to the light to see a beautiful forest like nothing you have ever seen before. It is teeming with life from animals to insects, plants and other beings. It feels alive, safe and peaceful. Look around and really take in its beauty.

You will notice another path, this time one covered with fallen leaves. Follow it for a short distance until you come across a clearing. In the middle of the clearing is a being, crystal, guide or entity you would like to commune with. Approach the being with an open mind and heart. Give your gratitude to the guide for being here for you and ask the questions you need to ask. Be respectful at all times and ask if there is anything you can give in return.

Once you have spoken with the guide, thank them and return the same way you came.

When you reach the doorway, walk through it and continue up the winding path until you reach the second door and then the third door, until you can see the light of the tunnel where it comes out at the tree roots. Climb out of the hole and let your eyes adjust. Thank the oak tree and walk through the field. As you do this you will become aware of your physical body once again. When you are ready, wiggle your fingers and toes and open your eyes. Journal your experiences in as much detail as you can.

CRYSTAL GRID ORACLE

CARDS

EMOTIONS

Black moonstone
Emotions, moon cycles, manifestation

Black moonstone, quartz lasers and points, coffee moonstone, natural citrine, black agate

Are you going through a particularly emotional time? You may be feeling as though things are getting out of control and you want everything to calm down. Moonstone can help you to deal with the intense energy of a full moon and/or your emotions. Black moonstone is also a very grounding stone, which makes it particularly useful when you are emotionally unbalanced.

We class emotions as being of the water element, that is, they are fluid and constantly in motion. Emotions = energy in motion. The moon as we know has an effect on water, governing the tides. We too are largely composed of water, so it makes sense we are also affected by the moon. Keen gardeners are also aware of the effect the moon has on plants. When you are working with emotions it is important to assess which chakra/s it may be coming from. If you have a block in a particular chakra it could be the overflow of built-up energy that needs to find a release.

Moonstone is also a perfect stone to grid your bedroom for a peaceful night's sleep, coupled with black tourmaline. Place a large piece under your bed and four tourmaline chunks in each of the four corners.

Citrine is a stone of abundance and manifestation. If you're feeling emotional it may be time to ask yourself: 'What do I want to create in my life with the help of citrine?' You may be feeling emotional because something is missing in your life or you are feeling out of control. Redefine what you want in your life and why. The citrine I use is an Australian citrine over morion. This combination is very grounding, so when wanting to manifest something in your life make sure you do it from a grounded place. If you are feeling scattered or not feeling centred, then ground. Go and place your feet on the grass and sit and relax. This is also called 'earthing', which has been scientifically shown to be beneficial in the human body.

EXERCISE

If you're feeling overly emotional at this time, take a moment to sit down and breathe. Ground yourself in any manner you like and bring yourself into the present. Feel the air on your skin, listen to birds or the wind through the trees and just be. When you need calm, grounding and centring is what is needed. Be the centre of your own grid and allow the energy to flow from you into the earth, where it can be transformed. Find the calm within yourself and watch your external world reflect it back.

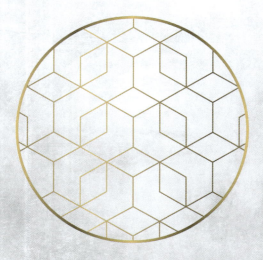

SPIRIT GUIDES

Celestite

Spirit guides, communication, direction

Celestite, quartz, optical calcite

Your guides are communicating with you now. Celestite helps you work with your higher chakras to enable you to communicate with your spirit guides. It brings calm and direction when you are in need. Your guides are always there no matter what the circumstance, and they are here to help you now. If ever we ask for help it is always given. You also need to listen to hear their answers. Spirit sends messages in many ways; they can be very subtle, just like the subtle colour of the stone. Discover how spirit communicates with you. Do you hear things? Do you just know things? You may see or smell certain things or receive images or words in your head. It is different for everyone, but the important thing for you is to trust in what you receive and how you receive it.

In order for you to receive any information or help you must also be open to receive. Take notice of whether you don't like to accept help when it is offered. Are you the kind of person who tends to push through alone and never let on that you are in need of help? Are you sceptical of anything? How do you take a compliment? This may be an indication that you are not open to receive.

Many people are good at giving but not receiving. If you're the type to always give of yourself but feel drained a lot by all of your efforts, it may be time for you to open yourself to receiving. How do you do this? Say the affirmation until you firmly believe it: 'I am open to receiving.' Allow yourself to receive from others; allow the help that you ask for to be given to you. Spirit has much wisdom if we only allow ourselves to receive.

EXERCISE

I find automatic writing is something that has helped me immensely over the years. It's as simple as journalling questions to be answered or having an open dialogue with my guides on paper. Don't worry if this all sounds foreign to you; give it a try anyway.

Start off by finding a space where you won't be disturbed, turn off your phone and get comfortable. Tell your guides you would love to speak with them, then start writing!

You might want to start off by writing 'Hello', then wait to receive a response. I get full sentences in my head, which I write down, but you might get images, feelings, smells or other messages. I find the language in which I receive the information is different from how I would normally write and that I am offered guidance I hadn't thought about.

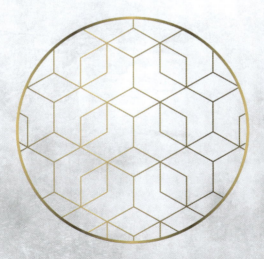

COMMUNICATION

Chalcanthite
Communication, goals, harmony
Chalcanthite, quartz, lapis lazuli

Communication is the key message here. Chalcanthite works with your throat chakra to help you communicate, and because it is a cluster of crystals it is especially good for communicating within a group situation or with a partner or friend. If you have drawn this card it is a time for you to express yourself, allowing the expression to manifest in the way that works best for you to get across what you have to say. Communication comes in many forms; whether it is verbal, written or through art, set a clear intention or goal and speak it into being. Let your true being express itself in an uninhibited manner.

Stand strong, speak your truth and be real. Push aside any cares of not being accepted, because if you project this you will receive it. When you are confident to speak your truth you will attract people who resonate with what you have to say. There will always be someone who does not believe what you have to say or does not like it, but their feelings are about them, not you.

When you have something you want to say but feel you cannot say it, you may create an imbalance in this chakra. This can lead to throat issues, such as a sore throat, a constant cough or the sensation of something stuck in your throat. If you refuse to say what you need to this can progress further, with the energy backing up into other chakras. If you truly feel you cannot speak your truth, write out what you really want to say on a piece of paper and burn it.

Keep a diary in which you can record anything that is on your mind. You could also channel this energy into painting or drawing. It doesn't matter if you feel you are not good at it; it is the act of doing that is the key here. No one needs to see but you, so just do and don't judge the final outcome. You never know: once you stop judging your ability you might find a satisfying new hobby!

EXERCISE

Wearing blue or finding a blue crystal or stone to carry with you can help shift the energies in your throat chakra. How do you want to express yourself today? What can you do, say or practise that allows you to be your authentic self and express what you want to express? You might want to journal the thoughts in your head or visualise yourself saying what you need to say. You might also like to ask spirit to give you the courage to say what you need to say or ask them to create a harmonious environment in which it can safely happen.

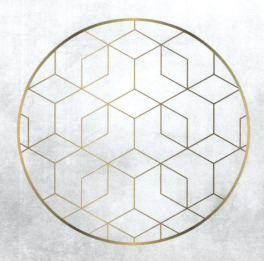

SELF-LOVE

Cobalto calcite
Self-love, unconditional love, self-discovery
Cobalto calcite, quartz

This is a simple grid, created to make the centrepiece the main focus: you. It is a stone of beauty, of unconditional love. This is a time for self-discovery, to learn more about you and to love yourself unconditionally without judgement. There is no need to compare yourself to others; you, too, have special qualities and it's time to show the world who you are.

By looking within and loving what you see, you give yourself permission to be you. When you love yourself you will draw others to you who will love you for who you are. Opening your heart centre will also bring great joy to your life. Sometimes just changing the way in which you look at yourself can change the way others also see you. Your strength and confidence need to come from within; only then can you truly shine.

Your heart chakra, the centre of your chakra system, is like your powerhouse to the chakras but is also the way in which you connect with the world around you. If you come from a place of love your world will be reflected back with love. If you come from a place of fear your whole energy system will contract and you'll draw more fear-based situations into your life.

The reason why so many wise men and women say to find love you must first go within is just that. In order for you to create a life that showers you with love you must first love yourself. When you love yourself you become more compassionate to others because you understand that you are not perfect, and you love yourself despite this and because of your imperfections. You can then apply the same compassion to others, and realise that you are here learning so you need to be gentle on yourself. Cast aside your judgement of yourself and know that you attract what you are. Be love, and you will attract love.

EXERCISE

Write a list of all the things you would love to do for yourself if you had the time and money. You can make this list full of little and big things, anything from going to your favourite coffee shop or reading a book in the sun with a cuppa to camping or travelling somewhere exotic. Really think about what brings you joy and what you have not given yourself in a long time.

Write out your list again, but this time order things into what you can do immediately and things that might be longer-term goals. This is now your self-love list. It is up to you to place yourself on your priority list and make time to give back to yourself. Take a bath, go on a holiday, have a massage or pamper yourself in any way you like and start making it a habit.

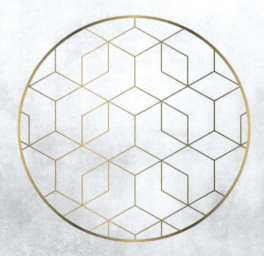

SOUL JOURNEY

Dumortierite
Soul journey, release, patterns
Dumortierite, kyanite, quartz

Dumortierite is a stone to assist you in discovering your soul journey. Do you know what you are here to do this lifetime? Have you always had a sense of purpose that you just must act on? Do you feel you may have brought in karmic life lessons or obstacles from past lives? Dumortierite and kyanite can help you find your answers. Dumortierite can assist with past life influences and kyanite will help release blockages, allowing more flow into your life. It helps you to tune in to your intuition, which is always the key to unlocking the answers to your questions.

It is time to pay attention to what your soul is saying, a time to evaluate what your purpose is in this lifetime, why you are here and what you feel you need to be doing. You may already be on your way, but maybe there are contracts or agreements that have been made before reincarnating that you realise do not serve you in this lifetime. Dumortierite can assist you to contact guides for help with these matters, which may lead to the removal of obstacles or give you new insight to keep you moving forward.

Remember, all you need do is ask for help. Your soul knows its way, so ask for guidance. Automatic writing can be very beneficial, or even just writing down questions for yourself to answer. Write the first thing that comes to mind and trust in what you write and receive.

EXERCISE

Dumortierite may not be a readily accessible stone, so meditating with this card and calling in the spirit of the stone may be the perfect solution. Remember that the physical stone is the manifestation of the energy that resides in it, so you can call on that energy at any time. Make sure you keep a journal or notepad handy for when you finish.

Set your intention for your meditation, which might be something such as gaining guidance on the next steps of your soul journey or finding your soul purpose. Keep in mind that your soul purpose will not always be completely revealed to you because there are steps you must learn along the way, so don't be disheartened if you don't know yet. There might not be one purpose and there may be many, or there could just be a common theme for your life such as creating peace wherever you go. Call on the crystal spirit to guide you, call on the spirit of kyanite to help you release what holds you from your soul journey and record all the information or images you get with your meditation.

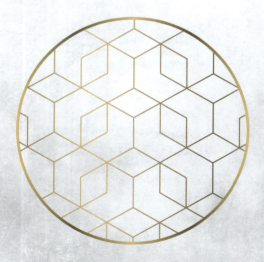

MANIFESTATION

Epidote

Manifestation, abundance, spiritual attunement

Epidote, atlantisite, quartz

Epidote is a stone of abundance and will increase or attract whatever you are sending out to the world. For this reason, this stone is not for everyone. If you are emanating fear and negativity epidote will bring more reasons to be fearful and more negativity towards you. In drawing this card, epidote is asking you to look at what you are drawing into your life at this present moment. If you are emanating joy and positivity you will attract more joy and positivity into your life. Gridding with epidote is therefore a very powerful tool. If you have a project or idea of what you want to attract or increase, epidote will help with this. Remember, pure thoughts and strong intent are key.

Atlantisite is placed here to bring in balance and calm. It is reputed to help you access past wisdom, which is always beneficial with manifestation. It is also a reminder about balance. Just like the yin-yang symbol, remember that what you may think is negative can actually be a gift from which you can learn.

Atlantisite is mainly serpentine and a beautiful stone to activate your kundalini and release any blockages that you may have when manifesting your desires. Keep in mind that sometimes you won't always get what you want when you try to manifest, because you may have blocks you need to work on first; this is what your grid may bring up for you instead. Always look for the reason why something manifests in your life. Everything is always as it should be.

EXERCISE

Is there something in your life you really want to manifest or change? In order to manifest you must be a vibratory match to draw it in. Get crystal clear on exactly what you want and how it would look like once you have achieved it, then create a space where you will not be disturbed and picture yourself already having achieved what you desire. Picture it in as much detail as you can, but also feel the emotion of it as though you are in the present moment with it. This is the key to manifesting, because this is how you change your vibration to match what you want to attract. You must feel as though it is the present moment and sit in a vibration of gratefulness.

Once you are finished you must be open to receiving and be aware of synchronicities that come into your life that will help you manifest what you put out to the universe.

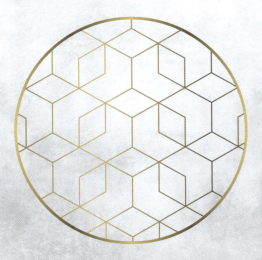

HEART PROTECTION

Pink fluorite
Heart protection, structure, balance
Pink fluorite, amethyst, quartz, optical calcite

Pink fluorite is a stone for your heart chakra. You may be in need of some heart protection. If you have recently gone through a break-up or lost someone you love, your heart may be vulnerable to even the slightest bit of stress. Your heart just needs some space and protection to heal. When your heart is out of balance it can affect all your other chakras, which can accentuate issues or just bring more sorrow. Let fluorite help protect you from any more undue stress, and allow it to bring organisation back to your life by helping you dissolve any negative energy that may have attached itself to you. This card may also indicate your heart is guarded and a wall may need to come down to let love in.

Pink fluorite will also assist you to stabilise your aura and aid in psychic work, as it operates with the third eye chakra; this is a perfect combination while working with heart issues. Allow your inner wisdom to help you through this situation. Maybe you are being guided to find what your heart truly desires. What makes your heart sing? Follow your intuition and come from a place of love, because when you do you will no longer need protection of any sort. Your heart will shine so strongly nothing will influence it.

This is a time to bring balance and structure into your world. Fluorite has a beautiful solid shape, so call on this crystal to help you bring structure and balance back to your life.

EXERCISE

If you're feeling vulnerable it's important to keep your energy protected. Pink fluorite can be a difficult stone to source, so call on the spirit of the stone to help protect your heart and aura. It is also a good idea to do a tree of life grounding exercise each morning until you feel strong again (see the 'How to use the cards' section). You can also wear stones that help ground you, such as hematite or petrified wood, or that deflect energy, such as obsidian or onyx. Black tourmaline is a favourite of mine to shift and also absorb and transmute energy. It is a great protector.

ANCESTORS

Preseli bluestone
Ancestors, wisdom, guidance

Preseli bluestone, quartz, optical calcite, 20 Celtic Ogham staves

Preseli bluestone is the stone from which the inner circle of Stonehenge is made. Each stave in the grid is one of the Celtic Ogham symbols, inscribed into its corresponding tree branch. This card can be used to connect with Celtic history and energy. Many people born in different parts of the world, such as New Zealand or Australia, may still carry the blood of their Celtic ancestors due to the history of these closely linked countries. Stonehenge is also believed to have once been a place where people came to honour and communicate with their ancestors who had passed over. Call on the help of your ancestors whatever their origin: they are always there to guide you. Somewhere that has called to you so silently, like a faint whisper, is now being heard.

Ancestors are not just the blood relatives in your family tree. When you call on your ancestors you are also calling on the collective consciousness of all those who have gone before you. Every spirit that has lived on the physical plane has returned to the earth, and you can draw on this collective wisdom at any time. Do you need answers or guidance? Draw on the wisdom of the ancestors, as they are always there if you care to listen. Go into nature, ground yourself and draw the wisdom up through your feet if need be or call to the ancestors in ritual/meditation, whatever that may be for you.

EXERCISE

Creating an altar where you can honour and contact your ancestors is a beautiful ritual. Altars can be as simple or elaborate as you like, but I like to keep things simple and uncluttered as it allows the energy to come through unobstructed by other energies. You need to find a space that is clean and will not be disturbed by animals or children. An altar in the garden, for example, will allow you to be in connection with the ground and nature.

Be intuitively guided as to what you want on your altar, and clean it and rearrange the items on it every few weeks to keep the energy from becoming stagnant. When I am at my altar I light a candle and some incense and call in whatever spirit energy I would like to work with. It's as simple as saying: 'Ancestors, please be with me, I need your guidance.' Meditate, sit and just be if that is all you feel you need to do, or ask for guidance on a specific question. Create an open dialogue with spirit and be open to what you receive, which could come to you days or weeks after asking. Whenever it comes, know that you have been heard.

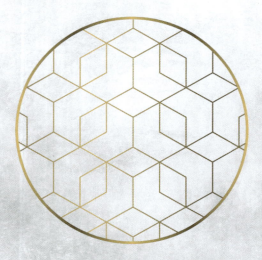

CLEANSING

Shungite

Cleansing, truth, ancient earth energy

Shungite, tourmaline, quartz

This is a time to cleanse. Shungite is a powerful cleanser, so if you have drawn this card it may be time to strip away all that is impure or that no longer serves you to reveal the truth. You may already be going through a big cleanse. Whatever the situation in which you find yourself, shungite will help you remove everything that is clouding the situation. You may need to cleanse the energy in a room or working space. Gridded in a room, shungite is very effective.

When coupled with black tourmaline it is a reminder to let it go and ground out energy you no longer need.

Shungite is reported to be around two billion years old, making it a very ancient earth energy stone. Because of its age it has experienced the many changes that have happened on this earth. Working with shungite can therefore help when going through changes of your own. Drawing on the wisdom of the stone and its ability to cleanse makes for a very deep change. Remember, you will always get through each situation you are presented with. You may not forget what happens to you, but you can choose to let it go and not hold on to its negative energy. Embrace change, let go of what you don't need in your life and carry on; you will become so much stronger for it. By letting go you give yourself room for new energy to manifest.

EXERCISE

Cleansing is a way of making room for fresh energy to move in. When you're feeling stuck, frustrated or in need of a way to move forward, cleaning your external environment is a great place to start. Look around your home, open old boxes, go through the cupboards and find everything you no longer need and donate it or let it go. When you make a shift like this in your physical environment it cannot help but be reflected within your internal environment also. Even the simple act of opening all the windows and smudging or lighting incense can allow for the movement of stuck energy. Completing unfinished projects is also a good way to make room for new energy.

TRANSFORMATION

Amethyst sceptre

Transformation, spiritual awareness

Amethyst sceptre, amethyst, quartz

Sceptres are very powerful crystals because they are actually two crystals in one, with one crystal having grown around the other. The main crystal penetrates deep into the other crystal, which represents getting to the core of the issue. Thus sceptres are great tools for allowing you to get to the root cause of an issue and make the necessary changes to rectify it, which means any sceptre is a powerful tool for spiritual awareness and transformation. It is also an excellent aid in energy work, as they are strong at generating and amplifying energy because they combine their energy and work together.

This particular sceptre is quartz and amethyst. Amethyst has long been a stone of the mind, so it will help with organising your thoughts to gain a deeper understanding of any issue you may be working with. This can indicate a time to look more deeply within to find what truly is the underlying issue. Related to your third eye chakra, it gives you in-sight. There is a bigger picture involved here that starts from inside. Great transformation always happens when you turn to the internal factors and decide that you truly have the strength to look at yourself. Meditation is a good place to start: still your mind and let your soul guide you.

EXERCISE

If you have a sceptre crystal it is perfect to meditate with, but it's okay if you don't as you can just meditate with the card. If you have an issue you need to go deeper into to find answers, call on the sceptre spirit and your guides and ask for their guidance. Always set an intention before you start and begin by relaxing and slowing your breathing. Breathe in the love from the crystal or card and breathe love back to the crystal or card. Repeat this cycle of sharing love between yourself and the crystal or card and take in any sensations you feel or see. When you have finished, record any experiences you had. Sometimes the answers won't come straight away but will be revealed at a later stage through certain circumstances.

INSIGHT

Iolite

Insight, re-energising, expression

Iolite, quartz

Iolite is a stone of spiritual insight, so this card is asking you to go within to find the answers you need. Iolite is a beautiful mix of blue and purple, which resonates with your throat and third eye chakras and thus your expression and connection to your spiritual guides. Sometimes you will try too hard to work everything out in your head, but now is the time to be open to receiving help from spirit.

Your guides step in when asked, so when was the last time you asked for their help? When did you last follow your intuition?

Follow what your inner guidance is telling you. Even if you think the situation is insurmountable, give yourself time to work with this grid and allow other possibilities to be shown to you. Ask your guides for their help and call in the iolite crystal spirit to strengthen this connection. Remember that your guides can see the bigger picture and you need to trust them.

Do you have a particular problem you need to shed some light on, or are you in need of assistance in focusing on what you need in your life? Whatever the issue may be, iolite is a beautiful stone to work with. It is an excellent aid for shamanic journeying or meditating to help you visualise, then allowing you to understand what you see. When you meditate or journey you may sometimes feel you're making it up, then your logical mind steps in. Trust is key when you're having a visual journey.

EXERCISE

Perform a shamanic journey to meet the iolite crystal spirit or a guide (see the 'How to use the cards' section). When you reach the spirit guide, ask for guidance on anything you wish to know. Make sure to record your experiences.

CROSSROADS

Chiastolite

Crossroads, protection, transmutation

Chiastolite, staurolite, quartz

Are you at a crossroads or torn in two directions? Have you found yourself in a position where you have to make a choice but are unclear which road to take? Sometimes it's hard when you're waiting for an answer to come but it just hasn't. Your feelings need to be your compass. If you feel joy, happiness or excitement when you think of an option you know which road to follow regardless of whether or not it is the logical road to go down. Follow the pull and see where it takes you. Your intuition is always right, and the more you learn to trust it the more you align yourself to your soul purpose. Your intuition is your own soul guiding you where you need to go. Remember that there is no wrong or right path to go down, only lessons to learn from. Sometimes we just need to make a decision and see where it leads us.

Staurolite is said to be a fairy stone. It is very grounding and can help with your connection to nature spirits. I have found this stone to be a particularly potent stone to get in tune with the four elements, as elemental beings can be powerful teachers when you reach out to them. Drawing this card may indicate it's time to make a grounded decision about something in your life, and having chiastolite and staurolite to aid you will be a good start!

EXERCISE

If you are at a crossroad, a good exercise to do with chiastolite or staurolite is to meditate and picture yourself walking up to that crossroad. See on the signposts the options or roads you can take. Do you feel a certain pull towards a specific path, or do you get the sense to not go down a certain road?

FUN

Orange calcite
Fun, emotional balance, energising
Orange calcite, citrine, quartz, optical calcite

Orange calcite is such an uplifting stone known to be beneficial in bringing light and laughter into your life. Are you in need of some fun? Have you been taking life too seriously, or do you feel like your emotions are like a roller coaster? Whenever you become very emotional and teary or have a creative block you should look to your sacral chakra. It is the water element chakra and therefore is attached to emotions, which is energy in motion. It is also the chakra associated with relationships with partners, finance and sexuality (females), and is the seat of your creativity. When there is imbalance in this area you need to bring back your emotional balance. Orange calcite is a perfect stone to help bring you some balance, inspiration and confidence. It will lift your mood and energise you and may even insert some passion in your life!

If you are experiencing a creative block, is it aligned with a relationship issue you may be going through? Sometimes you don't need to pinpoint what the situation is, but if you can recognise the signs of which chakra is involved you can use crystals accordingly. Remember that everything is energy, regardless of the situation that created the imbalance. Work at shifting or restoring energy and you will get results. When you shift into using your creative energy you move into a state of flow, which allows you to turn your thinking brain off for a while. It's important to make this switch and let your hair down: it's not only a fun thing to do but is also therapeutic!

EXERCISE

If you're having relationship or sexual issues or just need to break away from being stuck in a routine you could try using art as your therapy, as it works with the same chakra. Meditating with this card or carrying orange calcite with you will have the same effect. Be creative and wear something orange or eat orange foods if that works for you. Bring orange into your aura and have fun doing it!

DEEP HEALING

Azurite and malachite
Deep healing, energy, vision
Azurite, malachite, citrine, quartz, optical calcite

Deep healing is occurring now or may need to happen, and many changes may be occurring in your life at this time. Azurite and malachite are known to bring very deep emotions to the surface; it is necessary to release these emotions for healing to occur. Holding on to emotion can take more energy than just letting it go. It's like trying to hold a beach ball under water: it takes a lot of energy to keep it down, as it will keep trying to rise. Once you let it go the struggle ceases to exist. Just as you are going through these changes so, also, is the earth. In the way that azurite and malachite can look like a satellite view of the earth, this card represents 'As above, so below; as within, so without.' Allow yourself to release whatever has been buried, and know that as you heal so too does this healing occur around you.

Deep healing can only occur if you have the strength to look at yourself or your situations from a higher perspective and with compassion. Things don't happen to you, they happen for you. When you learn to grow from the situations you go through you can then understand that everything is an opportunity from which to grow. It doesn't mean that what happened was okay but rather that you have risen above it to a higher level of understanding and can look back with compassion and gratitude. Learn to grow from what you go through.

EXERCISE

It is always good to use clearing exercises when you're experiencing deep release. Let stress go from your body and aura and the space in which you live. Smudge your aura, use incense in your home and open the windows to let it all go. Spring clean or sweep away all that has become stagnant, leaving no stone unturned. Once you let go of stagnant and unwanted energy you make space for renewed energy. Let energy flow from you and into you. Open up to the exchange and allow yourself to become one with the flow that is continually happening around you. This will filter through every level of your being, and you will begin to understand how your external universe reflects your internal universe.

SOUL HEALING

Tangerine quartz

Soul healing, past-life healing, creativity

Tangerine quartz, quartz, optical calcite

Tangerine quartz is a powerful tool for healing the soul. It is said to help with trauma or shock of any kind, soul retrieval and past-life healing, and can show your soul how to see the positive in the lessons it learns. Shamans believe that when we experience trauma or shock a part of our soul fragments or remains stuck in that time of our life. If you have ever felt you haven't been the same since a certain event happened it could be a good opportunity to journey back to that event and bring that part of your soul home.

Sometimes you can also be reliving your past-life energy. Generally, if you keep doing something or a certain situation keeps happening and you have no idea why it can indicate past-life healing is needed. Working with a shaman can help you in this situation, as can calling on the healing energy or spirit of tangerine quartz. Tangerine quartz will help your soul heal and understand the lesson or gift in each trauma or learning experience. Tangerine quartz is also a beautiful aid to help with creativity and raising kundalini energy, which are both healing activities for the soul that allow you to release blockages and nurture yourself.

EXERCISE

Drawing this card may indicate it's time to seek out some healing from an external source. Perhaps find yourself someone who does soul retrieval if you feel drawn to it. If you are familiar with doing soul retrieval yourself, you might like to sit down and look at what patterns seem to be a recurring problem and do some internal work to discover their origin. If it stems from a particular event you could travel back in meditation or journey to yourself in that time and bring that part of yourself home, or reassure yourself that where you are now is a safe place, feel the emotions and let them go.

PEACE

Scolecite and tree agate

Peace, patterns, connections

Scolecite, tree agate, quartz, optical calcite

A time of peace is coming your way. Scolecite is an excellent stone to bring peace to relationships and help with improving connections within groups or help with networking with people. You may have been experiencing some negativity and are in need of finding inner peace, a place where you can step away and just breathe. You need to take time out for you and put yourself first.

Peace can come by finding your centre, just as the scolecite is placed in the centre of the grid. Find your centre, find your peace. Call upon scolecite when you need to find this peace or are having trouble creating space for yourself. It is especially useful for bringing in calm and peace within a group so you all work together and in flow.

Coupled with tree agate, like a circle of tree protection, this grid can instil a sense of security and strength to face any situation you may be experiencing. Be the scolecite in the centre of a ring of protection and find your inner peace again. When you find your centre you will know, as you will feel grounded and strong and your mind will be clear, enabling you to stand your ground and, most of all, feel peace. When you feel and radiate peace from within you will attract peace around you. Sometimes you need to let go of controlling what's happening around you and shift your energy to within.

EXERCISE

If you need to find peace or create it, take some time and find a tree to sit with where you will not be disturbed. The only thing you need to cultivate peace from within is intent. Close your eyes, slow your breathing and bring yourself into the present moment. Sense time slowing down around you and feel the sun or breeze on your skin. With every exhale, relax more and more of your body. If you feel any tension, let it go every time you breathe out.

Feel the presence of the tree you are sitting against. Sense how slow the tree's energy is compared with yours and bring yours into a vibrational match with the tree's. Feel the peace of slowing down from within and allow it to permeate every cell of your body. From there, push the vibration and your consciousness of this feeling out past your body as far as you can. Encompass the entire earth if you feel inclined. Once you are radiating peace from your entire being, bring your consciousness back to your centre and give your love and gratitude to the tree. You can then go about your day emanating peace and love all around.

CHANNELLING

Black phantom quartz
Channelling, transmitting, grounding
Black phantom quartz, kyanite, quartz, tourmaline

It's time for you to be very clear on what you wish to manifest. When you decide on what you want, draw on the energy of this crystal. The trans-channelling black phantom quartz will amplify what you need and transmit it. Its special configuration means it is the perfect tool to transmit or channel energy through its tip. Being in a cluster means it is harnessing the collective consciousness of all the crystals in that cluster, making it a powerful combination.

The black phantom, which gives it its grey appearance, will keep you grounded, coupled with the black kyanite and tourmaline. It is particularly helpful for those who are in service to humanity, allowing you to channel and tap into all that is. This is a very powerful card indeed, so while being clear on your intention you must also be prepared to receive what you ask for. Keep in mind that if you send out something full of potent energy you will receive the same back. Be clear with your intentions; ensure they are for the good of all. What you receive back can come in many forms, so be open to allowing this form to come into your life and being.

A wise person will not only accept what is given to them; they will also act on it. It is one thing to ask and receive, but the power of this gift ultimately resides in what you do with it.

EXERCISE

Channelling is a two-way street: just as we can send out what we want to the universe, so too can we receive from it. Automatic writing, drawing, singing and talking are forms of this. Try calling on your spirit guides to work through you and show you. Start with a blank page in your journal, a piece of paper or a canvas or just start singing, dancing or talking. Who cares if you feel silly at first or if nothing appears on the paper? The more you trust the process the more that will come through.

GROUNDING

Smoky quartz

Grounding, neutralising, earthing

Smoky quartz, citrine over smoky quartz, quartz, tourmaline

You may be in need of some grounding right now. It is easy to get caught up in spiritual and healing work, or having to do a lot of mental work or just doing too much at once. This can unbalance your energy, because your energy is being used by the upper half of your body. You may be feeling a bit spacey, you could be clumsy or things just may not seem to be quite right. This is a sure sign you need to ground, and working with smoky quartz or black tourmaline is excellent for this. Not only does it ground you, it also neutralises negative energy while bringing in calm.

Always remember to keep the balance. If you are doing a lot of mental or spiritual work that utilises your higher chakras, always balance this by doing something that uses your lower chakras or lower body such as gardening, earthing (placing your bare feet on the earth), doing something creative or using grounding stones such as smoky quartz or tourmaline. Carry the stones on you if you know you will be doing a lot of upper work, or wear a necklace or jewellery to help bring about balance. The more your vibrations rise the more important this simple exercise is needed. Grounding will make you feel more centred and in control of what's going on around you; you will be surprised at the impact of doing this. It will also help you feel more connected to Mother Earth and what she needs.

EXERCISE

The tree of life exercise in the section 'How to use the cards' is the perfect exercise to do anywhere. You can perform it in your mind's eye if you're somewhere in public, or if you're outside you might take your shoes off and do it with your feet touching the earth. You can also call on the spirit of smoky quartz or black tourmaline to help you ground and protect your energy field.

ANGELS
Selenite and angelite

ANGELS

Selenite and angelite
Angelic connections, light body
Selenite, angelite, quartz

This is a high vibrational card. Both selenite and angelite are crystals that work with angelic and higher consciousness. There are many aspects to this card, but mainly it is about gently opening up your crown or higher chakras to help with your telepathy and communication to a higher source. Selenite helps anchor your light body to the earth plane, which again is very necessary if you're working with higher energy. When you are anchored and protected you can truly trust in the wisdom and guidance you get while working with spirit.

Angelite will help you speak your truth from a place of higher being. Working with your throat chakra, which is your communication centre, angelite helps you communicate with the higher realms. Do you need higher guidance at this time, or do you wish to communicate to a loved one you hope is being cared for by the angels? Whatever the need, know that they communicate with compassion and love and always have your best interests at the forefront.

When you ask for help from the higher realms you will receive guidance from a higher perspective, one in which they understand the bigger picture involved. Sometimes you can't see the wood for the trees, situations where you just don't understand 'Why?' There is always a bigger picture, there is always a lesson and there is always a reason. Ask for guidance and take comfort in the fact that you are exactly where you are meant to be regardless of how it feels at this time.

EXERCISE

Selenite and quartz are readily accessible stones and relatively cheap to obtain for this exercise, but if you don't have them then work with the card and call in the crystal spirits to help you make the connections you need. Make yourself comfortable and close your eyes. Call in the angels and your guides to be with you, then ask them for their guidance or to show you a sign when they are near. This may come in the form of an image such as a feather, or it may come in the form of a sensation on your body or a sense that they are there. Take note of how they communicate with you so you will be able to recognise it in future.

PROSPERITY

Green garnet
Prosperity, confidence, fertility
Green garnet, quartz

Prosperity, fertility and success! Any form of abundance or success starts with a state of mind, so pay attention to your thoughts. Are you thinking future abundance, which will continue to keep that abundance in the future, or do your thoughts always turn to the lack of what you have in your life now, which creates more lack? Focus your thoughts on the now. What are you grateful for in this present moment, and what can you see that is abundant in your life?

Be aware that abundance does not always come in a monetary form. When you start to feel and appreciate the abundance you have in your life at the present moment, that is the point you start to draw more abundance to you. Green garnet can help bring a wealth of finances, and emotional, physical or creative pursuits. Either way, it is an awesome card to pull!

Green garnet also holds the qualities of red garnet, which is related to success in business, so if you don't have any green garnet on hand you can either meditate with this card or wear or use red garnet. You could try using other green stones with your garnet or use it on a green cloth, or you could use a clear piece of quartz and ask for the green garnet healing energy to come through it and be with you for whatever reason you need it for.

EXERCISE

Notice the image on the card and how the energy lines are vibrating out from the centre and magnifying as they get bigger and bigger: this is how you need to picture yourself when you are manifesting anything. You attract what you put out to the world, so if for example you wish to attract abundance you need to be a vibrational match to abundance and it will come to you. You do not have to go in search of anything you desire; you only need to be that vibration and it will be drawn to you.

Meditate with this card or a piece of garnet or quartz. Breathe in the love of the crystal and breathe love back to it. Create a cycle of flow in this manner between the crystal and yourself until you feel connected with it. Feel gratitude flowing through you. Feel it in the present moment, and when you are fully in the feeling push the feeling and energy past your physical body, letting the energy expand further and further out to the boundaries of your property and again further. Push this feeling of gratitude out past your suburb, state and country and then envelope the entire the earth with it. Feel the gratitude, feel the peace, feel the happiness. When you're ready, slowly bring your awareness and energy back to your physical being then wait to see how many other things to be grateful for come your way. Practise this as much as you can and you will certainly see a shift in your world.

BOUNDARIES

Calcite fairy stone
Boundaries, helper, earth anchor
Calcite fairy stone, green calcite, quartz, optical calcite

By drawing this card, which is about boundaries, you are being asked to look at the walls you have built up around yourself that now need to come down, or it may be indicating you need to set some boundaries for yourself or others. A time of new beginnings awaits, but you must be firm and respect yourself enough to make the changes.

Calcite fairy stones have a very strong connection with the earth and will act as an anchor when meditating or journeying. They are perfect stones to journey within and take a good look at what no longer serves you. Find your inner strength, set some boundaries, knock down a couple of walls and start afresh. Each calcite fairy stone has a unique shape: many look like people, so each stone has a specific purpose of its own. You can see by the concentric circles of this stone that it is about boundaries. Each one has its own story to tell, although all are earth anchors.

The stunning green calcite is always a welcome addition to any grid. It brings with it a sense of peace and love, reminding you that when you set your boundaries they must come from a place of love for yourself and others. Don't be unrealistic with your boundaries, or you might just be putting up a wall. Always be mindful of your actions or non-actions.

EXERCISE

Take a moment to reflect on what may be happening in your life at present. Are you feeling somewhat out of control in any area you sense you need to set some healthy boundaries for, or do you feel as though you've been too inflexible and need to bring some walls down? Setting an energetic barrier with your intent may be all that is needed to bring about change. Visit the tree of life exercise in the section 'How to use the book'. Doing this exercise with a calcite fairy stone would be beneficial, but if you don't have one you can call on its spirit. When you create the bubble around you say to yourself: 'Only love and light may enter this space, only that which serves my higher good. All negative ties and attachments that do not serve my highest good must leave now.' By setting this intent you allow that to permeate to your physical world.

REBIRTH

Menalite
Rebirth, lovers, heart
Menalite, morganite, aquamarine, quartz, optical calcite

Menalite is a stone of rebirth; a metamorphosis is happening! Even if you don't understand what it all means now, thank the universe for the opportunity for growth. With great change comes great reward: a new way of living, a new way of thinking, even a new lover or your soulmate? Menalite looks like a lump of clay being moulded, and so too can you undergo this kind of transformation. It can feel like everything has been tipped upside down and you don't know which way is up, but out of the clay a new form will appear. This form can remain the same or it can be remodelled again and again. It's up to you if you want to remain in this new shape or keep growing and changing as many times as you like in your lifetime. Just don't become stuck being something you're not; let change happen and see what you become!

Morganite and aquamarine make a perfect combination of blue and pink, male and female for attracting new love into your life. They form an equal union of the masculine and feminine or balance just like in the yin-yang symbol. It is such a gentle stone, and if you ever come across a piece carry it on you; you will feel love wherever you go. Exciting times indeed are coming if you have drawn this card, as you may now be well on your way to a lifelong soul connection or fresh opportunity as the new you emerges.

EXERCISE

Take a moment to think, feel and dream what you wish to become or manifest in your life. If you're going through a particularly difficult time picture what it will look like on the other side. Meditate with this card and call on the beautiful gentle crystal spirits that work through it. Picture where you want to be and feel the balanced energy of it having already manifested. Feel the peace of getting through and becoming the person you always wanted to be. Feel the gratitude of knowing everything is as it should be and all will be fine.

INSPIRATION

Chrysanthemum stone
Inspiration, harmony, fun
Chrysanthemum stone, golden calcite, quartz

Inspiration! It's time to light that spark and reach for the sky. It's time to be you, be creative, find your inner child and run with it. Chrysanthemum stone is a brilliant stone to inspire and bring a little joy into your life. Coupled with golden calcite and quartz, meditating on this card with this combination of stones will help you clearly see what you need to do to achieve your dreams.

Chrysanthemum stone looks like a burst of energy or the bloom of a flower. You may have been feeling a bit stuck or are taking life too seriously. Break free from the routine and discover new methods of getting away and doing things for you. Chrysanthemum stone will help you find your child-like qualities. Looking at life through the eyes of a child means viewing the world without stress, limitations and restrictions. You will realise how many more options there are that you were blind to. There are many more directions you can go if you allow yourself to think outside the box.

By asking for the wisdom of this stone to help you, you may get a spark of an idea or find help with beginning a new project. You may want to do things with others and get away, or you may throw yourself into creative endeavours. Bring yourself into the present moment and ask yourself, 'What do I need right now?' Whatever you choose, ask yourself this: 'Am I doing what I love?' It's time to be you and do what makes you feel alive.

EXERCISE

If you're stressed, tired or unwell it can be very hard to find inspiration, so drawing this card can mean it's time to look at why you're feeling that way in order to find the creativity you need. Giving back to yourself, resting when you're tired and self-care are important. You need to make space within yourself for illumination. This is your nudge from the universe to take time out for you and allow yourself to get back into flow. Write a list of all the things you could do, even if it's just a 15-minute break to be in the now or having a cuppa in the sun. Only when you make space for yourself will you allow inspiration in.

ANCIENT KNOWLEDGE

Smoky quartz record keeper
Ancient knowledge, grounding, portal

Smoky quartz record keeper, quartz, black kyanite

This is another grounding stone but one that also has ancient knowledge to share. Record keepers will allow you access to knowledge that is stored within the crystal. They can be seen as portals, and if you meditate with a record keeper it may permit you access to its hidden information. If you have a record keeper crystal it may be time to start working with it. Because they are stones of insight or looking within for answers, this shows you that it is time for you to do this yourself. All knowledge lies within, for you are connected to all that is. All information is available to you at any given moment if you seek and ask for it.

Meditating with this card may give you the answers or guidance you are looking for at this time. The fact that this crystal is also smoky quartz means it will help you remain grounded while working with these powerful energies. Black kyanite will help ground you but will also shift and move any energy that is necessary for your highest good. Allow it to assist you to remove your roadblocks so you can become a clear channel for higher information.

Seek out the knowledge you need, study a course or meditate on the record keeper to find some answers. Remember to look within, and equally important is to ask for help in finding the answers you are looking for.

EXERCISE

Record keeper crystals are characterised by little raised triangles on their faces, which can only be seen in a certain light. The triangles have very straight sides, and there may be one or many. Record keeper crystals are perfect to shamanic journey with, but if you don't have one you can still access the record keeper crystal on the card.

Perform a shamanic journey as in the section 'How to use the cards' to meet the crystal spirit. Shrink yourself down to find a door into the crystal and ask if you may enter it. When you're inside the crystal, offer your gratitude to the spirit that resides within and ask if it will show you the guidance or wisdom it has to offer. There may be many lessons to learn from the crystal, which you can come back to time and time again, or there may be just one main lesson to share. Be sure to record your experiences with the crystal as this is valuable information that may help you in the future if not now.

LOVE

Rose quartz generator
Love, relationships, self-forgiveness
Rose quartz generator, quartz

This is the stone of love, a gentle stone but a very powerful one. You may have drawn this card because you need some love, are looking for love or love has found you! Rose quartz may be asking you to look inside yourself; it is a time to let go of hurt and draw love to you. It has a subtle colour that teaches you to also be subtle when seeking love and be gentle on yourself. You will not find the true love you are searching for if you do not wholly love the person you are on the inside.

Rose quartz is a powerful stone to use when gridding. Create a loving, harmonious environment with it and carry a piece with you to bring peace and love to your person. Just by creating this loving environment in your home you are also giving yourself love. Choose more ways to give yourself this love and honour the beautiful person you are, and you'll find you attract people into your life who also reflect your own beauty.

Be mindful that when you are truly yourself you will find that special someone who will love you for you, who will love the person you had hiding from view. When you create the image of what you think people will want you create a false you and will attract someone who falls in love with this false reality. As you grow you reveal more of your true self. Let people fall in love with your true self, and the quality of your friendships and partners will mirror this beauty.

EXERCISE

Creating a love crystal grid within your home is a beautiful way to create a loving, peaceful area. You may have some rose quartz or quartz, or you can find something pink in your jewellery, a flower or something that represents love to you. Cleanse the area you intend the grid to remain in. This can be a small or large space; it is your intent that is key.

Place your pink item in the centre of the space and arrange any quartz pieces you have or other plants, flowers or leaves around the centre part. Centre yourself and call in your spirit guides and the rose quartz crystal spirit, or the spirit of whatever you have chosen for your centrepiece. Ask them to bring love to your space and amplify it. You could also breathe in love from the grid and breathe love back to the grid to amplify the energy of love. Make sure you fully connect with the feeling of love. Be love and radiate love and it will come back to you because you will be a vibratory match.

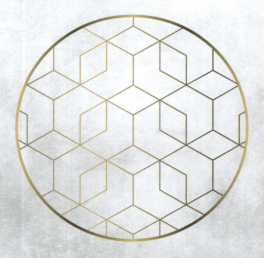

PROTECTION

Black tourmaline
Protection, strength, positivity
Black tourmaline, quartz

Does everyone seem to want something of you and you seem to be running on the spot and getting nowhere? Are you feeling super emotional and just want everyone to leave you alone? It could be time to put up some protection. This is a good indication that you are allowing outside energy to interfere with your own: you are taking on everyone's problems or feeling everyone else's energetic disharmony, and it is not doing you any favours. Picture putting a bubble around yourself and let all the negativity deflect and bounce off it.

Notice how the grid is created in this image. It is like a shield, and this is exactly what you need to do. It doesn't mean blocking people out or disassociating, it means you are saying 'My energy is my own, and you may not take it or enter into my energy if it is not for my highest good.' Black tourmaline grounds and absorbs negative energy and is one of my favourite stones, especially if I am feeling very sensitive. Use black tourmaline and feel your strength return as all the people and events that have been draining you dissolve away, leaving you with a sense of calm, strength and renewed purpose.

EXERCISE

For this exercise I suggest you purchase a piece of black tourmaline, which is a readily available stone. One small tumble stone is enough. This beautiful stone is one of my favourites, and when you have a piece you will understand why as it helps you feel at ease and move unwanted energy to restore your energy field to normal and gives you protection. It is a stone that just feels good in your hand, and buying a small necklace is beneficial. If you don't have the stone you can call on the crystal spirit at any time you need protection, such as when you are at a busy shopping centre or with a large group of people and feel vulnerable to external energies. When you're sensitive to energy this can be the perfect stone to call upon to keep you centred.

SOLUTIONS

Hypersthene
Solutions, relationships, discovery
Hypersthene (spectrolite), quartz, yellow mica

Here we have solutions and discovery, a grid resembling the medicine wheel that is based on the four directions and that many cultures around the world use. Each direction may be meditated or journeyed upon depending on what you are in need of answers to. Hypersthene will illuminate the way for you while also being an anchor to the earth. Remember that there are always many directions you can take in life, and each will have its own lessons. Hypersthene is a very calming and grounding stone that also illuminates the way forward. You must always make decisions in this manner, being calm and grounded. Yellow mica is also there to aid you in your problem solving.

You may wish to place the card in a specific direction of the medicine wheel and meditate on it to gain insight into an issue you are needing guidance with, or you may wish to discover what each direction on the wheel has to offer. Hypersthene has a beautiful inner sheen that reminds you of your inner reflection. What you receive in this world is a reflection of your inner self; see the beauty of who you are within and you will begin to see the beauty of the world around you. Discover who you truly are on the inside and you will find many answers to your questions in life. Call on the help of hypersthene to protect you from outside stressors so you can find solutions and your calm.

EXERCISE

What do you need to shine a light on? What questions do you need answered? Shamanic journeying with hypersthene or journeying to meet the crystal spirit can be beneficial. Follow the instructions for shamanic journeying in 'How to use the cards' and meet the crystal spirit. You might like to meet them in a medicine circle in a particular direction, or they may face a specific direction that you should take notice of. Ask a question and request the spirit's guidance. Trust what they show you and record what you experience. Keep coming back if you don't get anything immediately and see if the answers come from different directions.

LIGHT BRINGER

Candle quartz

Light bringer, soul purpose, earth healing

Candle quartz, quartz

Candle quartz is a light bringer. You have a soul purpose and you are here to help heal the earth. At times you may feel as though your light is not shining brightly, but at other times you may feel so bright that you illuminate everything everywhere you go. The role of a light worker can be very tough, and sometimes you may wonder why you ever decided to come to earth. Keep your chin up and continue to push forward. You may feel that you aren't really doing much, but know your purpose is great. Go forth knowing that every action, whether big or small, is making a difference; you are on the right track. Keep up the good work and continue to shine the light so others may find their way.

Candle quartz is a beautiful crystal to meditate with to bring light to a situation. You may want it to see into the darkest places of your self, or to find your soul purpose or more clarity on your current life path. It is a very gentle quartz when used this way. If you can't find your own light, draw on the qualities of this card and crystal. You can also use candle quartz to call on your guides and totem animals. They are present on your soul journey and will always remind you that you are not alone. Call on candle quartz when you need help lighting the way for not only yourself, but for others as well.

EXERCISE

If you're feeling like you're in a dark place it is time to find your light. Do this exercise at night when all is calm. If you have candle quartz hold it in your hands, but if you don't then call on the candle quartz spirit to be with you. Light a candle, and with your eyes open watch the flame. See the light dance and feel the warmth of the soft glow. See the beauty of one small candle and realise you, too, hold this beauty. You can shine when it's dark, you can give off warmth when it's cold and you can help show others the way by shining a light ahead. Never give up hope, because sometimes you need the dark in order to see the light. Ask the quartz spirit to help you shine a light and see the light or be the light. Know that you are in the here and now and this is where you will find peace.

COMPASSION

Ajoite

Compassion, high vibration, communication

Ajoite, aquamarine, quartz

Ajoite (pronounced *ah-hoe-ite*) is a very high vibrational crystal. You may be in need of some guidance, especially if you are a light worker. Use ajoite when you need to tap back into the source and seek answers on a higher, spiritual level. It elevates you to a realm where you can communicate freely with spirit, then aids you in communicating this information on the earth plane with compassion. A stone of spirit communication, it is perfect for spiritual teachers.

Having compassion for another means you have reached a level where you can see a situation for what it is. You see the bigger picture and all judgement has been removed from the situation; this is the sign of a true spiritual teacher. Reaching this state of compassion is ultimately our goal. For each lesson you learn there are others also learning the same lesson, and you will continue to keep learning lessons until you die. This is how you grow and become more spiritually aware. It isn't a race: we are all here to help one another and we all learn what we need to when we are meant to. When you start to view the world with compassion rather than judgement the world becomes a much better place, and your interactions with others will shift accordingly.

Ajoite is a rather expensive stone. If you don't have a piece you can still draw on its energy by asking for its help. Remember that there are no boundaries when you work energetically; we are all connected and need only call on the energy we need for its help. I also love the number it fell on, 29, which is 2 + 9 = 11 and thus a master number.

EXERCISE

If you find yourself in a difficult situation or see that you're being judgemental you might like to work with the ajoite spirit, or you might just like to raise your vibration to a state of compassion for the pure enjoyment of being uplifted. Meditate with this card or use a piece of quartz to help call in the crystal spirit. Ask the spirit to help you see from a higher perspective in order to understand the lessons you need to learn from your situation, or just sit and bask in the higher state of compassion and know that by raising your vibration you draw to you the same higher frequencies. If you're unable to work through a situation in your head, raising your vibration higher will draw what you need to you in the physical world.

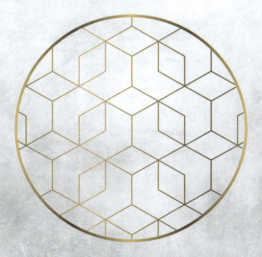

PASSION

Ruby record keeper

Passion, shield, courage

Ruby record keeper, quartz, garnet, optical calcite

Ruby is a stone that stimulates the base, sacral and heart chakras. Draw on it when you need courage or strength. You may have exhausted yourself doing too much or are battling through some life changes. It's time to recharge your batteries with ruby and stimulate your creativity as well as your vitality. It's also time to bring passion back to your life while ensuring you remember to nurture yourself. You need to give your body the right nutrition, so when you find your passion for something you have the physical stamina to see it through. Being closely associated with the base chakra, ruby reminds you to look after yourself physically. Ruby can also stimulate kundalini energy, so if it's passion you're after then ruby is your crystal.

As well as the beautiful qualities ruby brings the crystal in this grid is also a record keeper, a keeper of ancient information. Is it answers you seek? Meditating with record keepers can help you discover universal truths. Do not go into meditation with a specific question in mind; let whatever information is in the crystal come to you. You may be surprised by what you receive, but know it is exactly what you need at this time.

EXERCISE

Record keeper crystals are perfect for shamanic journeys, but meditating with them is as effective. If you do a shamanic journey, shrink yourself down so you can enter the crystal and learn what it has to offer you. Meditating and asking the crystal spirit to show you what wisdom it holds will allow you to be open to its teachings. Do whatever works best for you, or maybe try both! Another way you can support your base chakra is by eating good food and red foods such as beetroot.

NATURE'S CYCLES
Malachite pentagram

NATURE'S CYCLES

Malachite pentagram
Nature's cycles, protection, devas

Malachite pentagram, quartz, aventurine, black agate,
optical calcite

The pentagram has long been a symbol of balance between the five
elements – earth, air, fire, water and spirit – and how they work in
harmony with each other. Traditional Chinese medicine also uses it
to represent their five elements: earth, metal, water, wood and fire.
Drawing this card means it is time to find balance within yourself
and reconnect with nature. Listen to what your body is telling you

and what others see in you. Get in touch with nature by helping the environment, learning about herbs, going for bush walks, gardening and so on. There are so many ways in which you can get back in touch with nature that will allow you to become more in tune with yourself.

By holding or meditating with malachite you can start to become attuned again. Remember you are also part of nature; there is no separation. Being a green stone means malachite also works on the heart chakra, which is how you connect with nature and the world around you. If you wish to make contact with nature spirits such as the fae you need a pure heart. You cannot trick them; they see through all your guises.

Malachite is an extremely beneficial stone for bringing issues and toxic thoughts to the surface, which could lend it to being an unlucky stone for some. If you truly wish to grow and let go of that which does not serve you or is sabotaging you then work with malachite.

EXERCISE

Keeping a journal of the year is something I find incredibly rewarding. Not only do you gain a better understanding of nature's cycles, you learn to see what is around you and the timing in which certain plants, insects and animals show themselves. This simple act of observing the world can offer you more than you can imagine. Become in tune with your surroundings, get to know what plants are growing where you live and learn to read the patterns of the flowers and what insects they attract.

BALANCE

Shaman stones
Balance, dissolving blockages, alignment
Shaman stones, quartz plus an unknown stone (arrow)

Shaman stones come in pairs, the female being the smooth stone and the male having protrusions. They are incredibly grounding stones that lend themselves to clearing emotions and dissolving blockages within the lower chakras to align and balance the masculine and feminine aspects within you. In this grid both are joined, but the masculine is giving its strength to the feminine.

It is very easy for females to try to take on the masculine role – sometimes it is a necessity to get through life – but remember to nurture the feminine qualities you have. Everything needs balance in this world, like yin and yang. Each quality needs its equal but opposite partner. Showing your feminine side may make you feel vulnerable, but if you have a balance of both masculine and feminine you will also find strength. The same is true for males who feel it is not masculine to show their emotions, love or caring side. Showing a feminine nurturing side is not a weakness. There are strengths and weaknesses in both energies, and it is up to you to find the balance of both within yourself. Strength comes from having the courage to show every aspect of yourself and the confidence to be who you want to be.

Shaman stones, as the name suggests, are used by shamans to ground or anchor them to the earth when they journey, among many other uses. They are highly protective, as their make-up suggests. They are a strong iron-ore rock surrounding a soft inner core of sandstone, making them excellent stones for protection.

EXERCISE

If you're feeling out of balance, holding a shaman stone in each hand can return your balance and help you find your centre again. If you don't have these stones, call on their energy or use the card to meditate with. When meditating, bring your awareness to your physical and energetic body. Do you sense whether you're out of balance in some way? Can you feel whether the left or right side of your body feels different? Generally, your left side is the feminine side and your right is the masculine. Do you feel the energies are working together mutually or is there a disconnect? Call on the crystal spirits to help you balance the masculine and feminine and allow yourself to let go.

Shamanic journeying is also extremely beneficial with these stones. They can be used to anchor you on your journeys and also aid in protecting you.

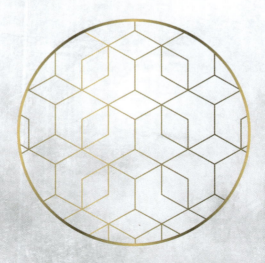

TRANSITION

Botryoidal lepidolite
Transition, absorption, stabilisation
Botryoidal lepidolite, quartz, amethyst, optical calcite

The stone of transition, botryoidal lepidolite indicates a time of restructure and re-organisation of old patterns and beliefs. It may be a stressful time for you, but it is time to bring calm and harmony into your life. Trust that with transition come new ways of thinking and being. The upheaval is all part of the process, so there is no need to worry; everything is as it should be. Allow yourself to flow through this transition, knowing that old patterns will be transformed into new ways of thinking and being for your higher good. What no longer serves you is being transformed into something that will, so you can bring a sense of stability back into your life. This in turn will also help with returning your emotional balance. Meditating with this stone or card, or even just asking for the energy of lepidolite to be with you at this time, may bring a sense of calm.

Lepidolite is known for its ability to relieve stress. Being a purple stone, it helps with your mind or third eye chakra to reduce obsessive thoughts. It is also used near computers to absorb the electromagnetic energy they create. Let lepidolite alleviate your stress and bring calm to your body and your environment. It will clear blockages that are holding you back so you can move forward uninhibitedly. It's time to balance your emotions, de-stress, focus and achieve your goals with or without help from others. You can do this; you are doing it! Trust in the process and you will be rewarded.

EXERCISE

Lepidolite can be a relatively easy stone to acquire and you don't specifically need to get the botryoidal type. If you don't have the physical stone, call on the crystal spirit to help you through the transition. Your state of mind is important, so if you're going through a particularly tough time say 'Thank you'. By doing this you are acknowledging that whatever is happening *to* you is happening *for* you. You may not understand now, but it will become apparent later and then you will realise it was a gift. When you approach transitions and lessons in this way it will give you courage to get through it instead of being swept up in it.

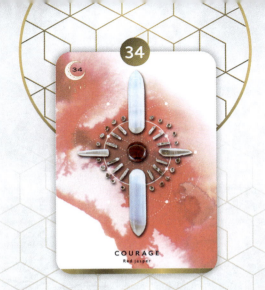

COURAGE

Red jasper
Courage, insight, detoxification
Red jasper, selenite, quartz

Red jasper coupled with selenite is a very balanced combination, because red jasper is a stone that works on the base chakra while selenite works on the higher chakras. This enables you to bring in the wisdom of the higher realms and ground it in the physical realm. Red jasper helps with insight, which is strengthened by selenite to also receive information from spirit. Red jasper is known as a stone of courage, so it may be time for you to stand up and be courageous.

See how the selenite looks like a sword? Strength and valour are needed at this time. Ground yourself and ask for guidance from spirit. Trust that the insight you receive is exactly what you need right now and act with strength. Plant your feet firmly, strengthen your boundaries and stand by your decision.

Red jasper is also known as a powerful detoxifier and is said to work on the blood and circulatory system. It may be time to discover deeper self-sabotage patterns that are holding you from standing in your own power. Remove the obstacles, go forth with a renewed sense of courage and trust in your ability to stand on your own. Know that every step of the way you will be protected by red jasper.

EXERCISE

Strength and courage come from within, although sometimes working on the physical can instil these in us as well. Being a base chakra issue, this card asks you to look at what food and nourishment you put into your body. Do you feel physically strong? If not, it's time to nourish your body in order to nourish the soul. Your internal and external environments will always be a match because they are both manifestations of your energy. Become aware of the things you put in your body that make you feel weak such as sugar and alcohol. Call on spirit to help you find your strength and courage, and work on your base chakra by using red stones or clothing or meditating with this card. You could also do a meditation in which you focus on your base chakra and ask it what it needs.

RELEASE

Tektite and ulexite

Stellar communication, release, insight

Tektite, ulexite, quartz, optical calcite

Tektite is meteoric glass formed by a meteorite impact with the earth. The impact melts the ground, splashing it over distance and speed so that it forms into irregular shapes. You can imagine the speed at which the original meteorite hurtled through the atmosphere and the great distance it had travelled. Tektite is here to help you realise all the lessons you have picked up along your journey. Have you accumulated a wealth of knowledge over your lifetime/s, or is it time to leave all that no longer serves you behind and move forward? You are an amazing being and should be proud of how you have learned from your past, which has helped you know how to navigate and focus on where you are going. This makes it a stone of transformation, whereby the stone has literally combined with the earth and become something new; it is a beautiful balance of 'As above, so below.'

It is also a stone that can aid telepathy, and because it comes from outer space it is believed to aid communication with other worlds and beings. It is an aid to gain knowledge from higher sources.

Ulexite, or TV stone as it is sometimes referred to, is an excellent companion to tektite. It is a stone to help with clear seeing, whether that be into a problem, seeing into others or seeing over distance; it will help magnify whatever you are searching for. If it is placed on your forehead when you are meditating it may assist in giving you further insight and clarity in these matters. This is a powerful combination to bring any issue to the surface that you wish to let go of while also creating a layer of protection around you.

EXERCISE

There are many exercises you can do with this card, depending on what you're looking for. You can work with tektite to help you release or transform anything that no longer serves you or to make contact with the higher realms. Shamanic journeying is incredibly powerful with this stone and will help you access the upper world, while also keeping you grounded. You can use the card to raise your vibration when needed or ask the crystal to help you transmute energy into something more beneficial for you.

CLARITY

Herkimer diamond
Clarity, attunement, potential
Herkimer diamond, quartz sceptres, quartz

A time of clarity awaits you. Your questions have been heard, you have asked for answers and the situation is about to become crystal clear. It may also be time for you to be clear with your intentions. When you know what you want your thoughts send out a clear intention to the universe for the law of attraction to manifest it for you. Herkimers are small crystals, but very powerful ones. So, too, can a small but clear intent be powerful.

When you feel stuck around a situation or are not manifesting what you want in your life it could be a time when you need to assess exactly what you want and how it would look if you already had it. Sometimes what you think you want isn't what you want at all. Sit down and really think about what you want your life to look like, or the job, car or partner you desire. Whatever it is you really wish to have, picture yourself having already achieved it and then feel if that is really what you want. Once you have the picture clear in your mind the universe can bring it to you, because if you don't know what you want the universe can't bring it to you.

Herkimers clear your chakras and remove blockages, which helps to activate your light body and discover your soul purpose by helping you to release past-life trauma. They are strongly associated with your crown chakra, which is your connection to your soul purpose and the higher realms. It is a good tool to meditate with or ask for guidance when in need.

EXERCISE

Herkimer diamonds are also known as the stones of attunement. If you wish to attune to your environment or as a healer to attune to your client's energy, use a Herkimer diamond. Wear or carry one when you're speaking in public, ask to be attuned to the energy in the room and call on spirit to work through you. Meditate with Herkimer to gain clarity and higher insight around issues you might have. They are extremely high-vibration stones, so if you start to feel a bit scattered or ungrounded remove the Herkimer from your energy field or use black tourmaline to ground you.

THE PATHWAY

Petrified wood
Pathway connectedness, direction
Petrified wood, citrine over morion, quartz, onyx

Petrified wood is a fossil that is formed when minerals, usually silica but sometimes other minerals such as opal, get within and between the cells of natural wood that has fallen. Parts of the tree thus turn into very hard stone that displays the lines of the tree rings and grain within it. It is quite common and can come in many different colours.

Trees are great teachers: not only are they wise from the aeons of knowledge they have accumulated throughout the years, but they are a necessary part of our survival.

Once when I was working with petrified wood, I visualised being in a dense forest with no apparent path to follow. I didn't know which direction to take, then I heard a whisper in my ear that said: 'Make your own path.'

Petrified wood shows you a new way of thinking is here. You may be so accustomed to treading the path of someone before you that you don't realise you are able to make your own path for others to follow. You don't need to fit into a box: you can be anything you want and create a life beyond your wildest dreams if you choose to do so.

Creating a new path always has its obstacles, but the rewards can be great. Not only do you gain a sense of accomplishment, but your success will allow others to follow in your footsteps. What legacy do you want to leave on your path? What do you want to be known for and how do you want to help others? Showing the way for others while you create your dreams is enough in itself. There is no one direction you need to go; it is entirely up to you where you start and where you end up.

Just as all the trees are connected under the earth through their vast root networks, so are you connected. You can ask the trees to help you with your issues, and your wishes can be sent through their entire network to wherever you need them to be heard. Learning more about Celtic trees can be an invaluable tool for expanding your awareness and creating a deeper connection with trees. It may be time for you to start working with them.

EXERCISE

When you are looking for direction or help, you can meditate with a piece of petrified wood or this card, or call on the trees or sit under one and ask for guidance. You could visualise your wish flowing as energy into a tree's roots and then under the ground where all the roots are connected with each other, spanning the globe. See your wish being transferred into light and being heard all around the world. Remember to always thank the trees for their help and guidance. Once you have been shown the way it is up to you to walk the path.

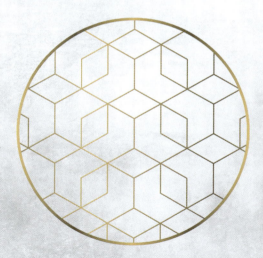

THE SEEING EYE

Septarian

Awakening, grounding, protection

Septarian, black onyx, amethyst, quartz

Septarian nodules, which are also known as dragon stones, are around 50 to 70 million years old. They were formed from sea shells and bones and molten sediment from volcanic eruptions. Over time and as the water receded the nodules cracked, exposing the aragonite, calcite and limestone crystals that had formed within. What was unseen is now seen. Things that have remained hidden for a long time or were unnoticed are now coming to light. Awareness at a higher level is being shone on a situation that has escaped attention.

Septarian is an ancient stone of awakening with the ability to help you to not only ground yourself, but to experience an inner breaking open that reveals the beauty of what you have inside. It is a time of having your eyes wide open to what is around you, of lifting the veil that had concealed all that was hidden but needed time to form into what it now is.

Connecting with this stone can bring great change. With great change means new ways of seeing, being and of letting old behaviours that no longer serve you be replaced by fresh ones that do. This also means you need to allow yourself to be open to new things.

The seeing eye can also represent protection from those who may be directing negative energy towards you whether on purpose or not, which can come in the form of jealousy, anger or even misunderstandings. With the aid of black onyx you can reflect that energy back to the person without it affecting you. When you stand in your power and are grounded and centred this kind of negative energy can't attach itself to you, so raising your vibration to a higher level is key.

EXERCISE

Carrying this stone with you can create a shield of protection, as well as assist you to heal your emotional body from the inside. Meditating with this card can also help you to connect to its deep earthen medicine as well as that of the water, fire and air elements.

PROPHECY

Prophecy stone
Prophecy, guides, answers
Prophecy stone, amethyst, quartz, optical calcite, onyx

Prophecy stones are very unique and mostly come from the White Desert in Egypt. They are pseudomorphs, or minerals that take the form of other minerals. In this case limonite and hematite take over a marcasite and pyrite structure, leaving the original shape intact but forming with a new molecular structure.

Drawing this card could indicate that some searching in the future may provide answers to the questions you seek in the present moment. It may be time to call on your guides or do some meditation or shamanic journeying. This card also shows you that the decisions you make now will take you where you are meant to be in the future, so it is up to you to decide where you need to be so you can take the necessary steps to get there.

Prophecy stones have very high vibrations that help ground energy. They also work with the third eye and are therefore useful in meditation and astral or visionary work. Formulate a question that needs answering and ask for answers from a higher source. What you can't see in the future are all the possibilities and paths that lie before you. Your future self and your guides can see these paths and the decisions that lie before you. There may be many paths to choose from, but it is you who needs to make the decision.

EXERCISE

Shamanic journeying to meet your future self can be an extremely beneficial tool to help you through current situations or to give you guidance on the next steps to take. Meditating with this card or stone and asking for guidance to come to you would also be beneficial.

EXPRESSION

Hemimorphite
Expression, communication, joy
Hemimorphite, quartz, topaz, aquamarine

Hemimorphite is a zinc-containing mineral very similar to smithsonite. They were once thought to be the same; however, they do have a slightly different chemical make-up. Hemimorphite is most commonly seen in a beautiful calming blue colour, but it can also be found in other colours.

There are many ways to express yourself through communication. You express who you are through the way you dress, the car you drive and the words you speak. Hemimorphite enhances your ability to communicate in a positive and joyful way, as it works closely with your heart chakra. When you communicate from a place of love, understanding and joy you cannot but help flow that energy to other people, and when this happens it allows others to communicate in the same way. Accordingly, hemimorphite is commonly used when walking into situations of conflict, as it allows you to speak with softer words and a sense of calm.

Hemimorphite is a terrific stone to have when working through relationship difficulties where good communication is needed, as it allows both parties to truly open up and be vulnerable. It can also aid you when your emotions are overwhelming, allowing you to release or understand them better and bring a sense of calm.

Hemimorphite helps you express yourself at a higher vibration, making it easier to communicate with your higher self and your guides and angels. When you lift your vibration in any situation you see things from a different perspective, one of understanding for where a person is at and the lessons you are learning, and one of love and compassion.

EXERCISE

If you're feeling emotional because there is something you need to say or a conversation that needs to be had, ask for hemimorphite to be with you. Carry a stone or place the card near you. Call on the energy of the stone and your angels, guides and higher self to be with you while you communicate what needs to be said. Be guided to having a gentle conversation, opening your heart and truly expressing yourself from a place of vulnerability. If you are doing this exercise by yourself you may like to write it all down then read over it, digest it and burn or bury it.

WISDOM

Turquoise
Wisdom, protection, power

Turquoise, aventurine, quartz, Herkimer diamond

Turquoise has been worn for centuries as a symbol of wisdom and protection. It can display stunning blues to blue green and yellow green and is usually accented by another host rock flowing through it. The striking blue comes from copper within the stone, which is accompanied by aluminium, while other shades indicate there are other minerals within the turquoise. It is quite porous and soft and can absorb the oils from your skin over time and change colour.

Turquoise has been used for centuries as a powerful protection stone as it helps you find your courage when you are going into battle.

It is time to listen to the wisdom within your soul or from someone who carries knowledge from years of living on this plane. Wisdom is gained through life experience, and from situations you go through in order to learn something valuable. You will keep repeating patterns until the lesson is learned, so you must ask yourself what you need to learn from what is being presented now. This plane of existence is one big hologram to grow from, which means that things are not happening *to* you but are happening *for* you.

When you learn to view every situation from a different angle and understand that they occur so you can grow, you can then take a different course of action or re-action. Although you may not be able to control the people you come into contact with, you can control how you react to situations. When you look at an issue from a higher perspective or from a position of understanding, the situation will no longer have control over you: you will accept that it is as it should be and move on.

When you don't allow yourself to be weighed down by situations out of your control you stand in your true power. You push through your fears to find yourself in a place of love, joy and gratitude.

EXERCISE

When you need courage, wisdom or power, call in the spirit of turquoise or carry a stone with you. While wearing a necklace or ring with turquoise, ask its spirit to create a layer of protection around you and give you courage, and ask for it to share its wisdom with you.

C O N N E C T I O N

Diopside
Connection, nature, centring
Diopside, epidote, quartz, onyx

Diopside can be found in many different colours but is normally seen in a beautiful deep yellow green similar in appearance to dioptase. It is chromium that gives the green colour to both of these stones as well as many other crystals, although they are completely different in their chemical composition.

Your connection to your external environment relates to your heart chakra: if your heart has been hurt you naturally protect yourself by guarding your heart and vulnerability. When you do this it can affect your ability to receive and therefore your ability to give. The greatest gift you can give yourself is making a strong connection with nature, because you are part of nature. When you strengthen the connection you will also find a better connection with yourself.

You can learn so much by observing and being in nature. Are you actively making the connection? Are you actively doing your spiritual practices to make stronger connections with spirit, animals or plants? When did you last place your feet on the ground and just be? Is your chest constricted and your breath shallow? These can be indications that you need to relax, breathe deep and connect more wholly through your heart centre and be open to receiving. Especially do this when you are in nature, but if you can't get out and about find a pot plant, shrub, tree or patch of grass to reconnect with.

Whenever you feel as though you don't know which path to take or which way to turn you may feel lost or that you have no direction. This tells you that you need to reconnect. Connect to nature, connect to your higher self, open your heart centre and let the flow begin.

EXERCISE

Find a practice that fits in with your routine, where you can actively make a connection with nature for at least 15 minutes a day. This might be as simple as having your morning cup of tea while sitting outside, not looking at your phone and just being. Deeply breathe in the air, the life around you, and see beauty in the smallest things. You might like to create an altar either inside or outside where you sit and just be and thank spirit for being with you or declare what you are grateful for.

HEART CENTRE
Watermelon tourmaline

HEART CENTRE

Watermelon tourmaline
Heart centre, higher vibration, heart medicine
Watermelon tourmaline, pink and green tourmaline, epidote, quartz, optical calcite

Watermelon tourmaline is a beautiful combination of pink and green tourmaline in concentric bands. It is normally seen with a vibrant pink centre and green outer, just like a watermelon. The stone in the centre of this grid can be called a reverse watermelon as it is green in the centre with a pink band.

Resonating with your heart chakra, watermelon tourmaline of either pink or green is good heart medicine. Your heart chakra is the centre of your chakra system and is the centre from which you interact with your external environment. When you allow this centre to be open and free flowing you allow people, events and gifts to enter your life, and you allow yourself to be connected with something much greater than yourself and will understand that you are connected with everything.

When you work from your heart centre you work from a place of love: the universal energy that everything responds to. Animals, plants and people all respond to love, which is important for the planet to progress. When you give love freely and see things from a place of love you receive the same back. Love is a very high vibration, and the more you attune yourself to this vibration the more it will lift your whole being and external environment to match.

When you love you radiate love, which lifts the vibrations of those around you. Those who lack love need it the most, so be kind and understanding, love yourself and others and watch your external life shift to match your vibration. It may be time to open your heart again. When you have been hurt you shut down this centre and become withdrawn, which in turn blocks your ability to receive. Learn how to open your heart centre again so you can let love in.

EXERCISE

For this meditation exercise, sit comfortably where you will not be disturbed. If you have any watermelon tourmaline or any green or pink stones they would be great to meditate with, although it is not essential, or you can place this card in front of you. Close your eyes and become aware of your breathing:

do you feel constricted around your chest or are you breathing shallowly? Be aware of any tightness in your body and let it go, then start to breathe more deeply. Really let your chest expand to start with and then breathe deeply from your core. Picture yourself breathing in and out of your heart space, and breathe in the love of the crystal energy and breathe out love. Do this as often as it takes to open up your heart space.

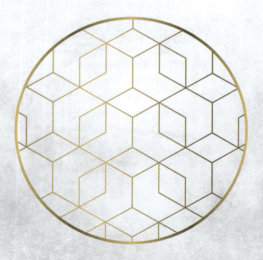

GROWTH

Quartz stalactite

Growth, wisdom, communication

Quartz stalactite, quartz, lapis lazuli, selenite

Quartz stalactites form over a very long time, as water under certain pH conditions in a cave drip and leave mineral deposits hanging from the roof – a stalactite – and drip to the ground below to create a stalagmite. The formation becomes a collection of many little terminations that are stuck to a main shaft or crystal of quartz that point in every direction.

A quartz stalactite is a beautiful symbol of growth, represented by the many drops of wisdom that have been accumulated over the years. It is a symbol that indicates you are growing from your circumstances or there is something you need to understand so you can grow from it. You do not wake up wise; you accumulate knowledge from all of the many situations you find yourself in throughout your lifetime. This accumulation of knowledge makes you stronger as you grow, so you must thank every situation that is presented to you even if you can't see the reason at the time. If you remember that things don't happen *to* you, that they happen *for* you, you can take a step back from a situation and know there is a lesson in there from which you can grow.

As a collective on this planet we are all learning the same lessons on different time scales, but sometimes we have lessons or shifts as a group collective. When you are faced with issues you use collective knowledge to make your decisions on how to move forward, but sometimes if the knowledge is not there or there is too much conflicting information to make a decision you need to trust your intuition. Only then can you move forward through uncertainty. The day may never come when you have all the answers or they may come way too late, so instead ask yourself how you can grow from your current situation.

EXERCISE

If you find yourself in a situation you don't understand, ask yourself what you can learn from it and how you can grow. Write down all the ways in which you can see the positives from the situation. If someone you knew was going through the same situation, what advice would you give them by looking in from the outside? This may help you see things in a different light.

BALANCE

Magnetite
Balance, wisdom, communication
Magnetite, onyx, quartz, citrine

Magnetite is an iron ore that is ferrimagnetic; that is, the atoms within it have opposing magnetic moments. It is attracted to magnets and can also become one. The name derives from it being the most magnetic of all minerals on earth. What are you drawing into your life or have an affinity to manifest? When you come to understand that you attract everything into your life you can use that to your advantage: are you attracting negativity, positivity, wealth or lack? When you look at what you are attracting you can look at how to change that if necessary. If you're attracting lack you must find the abundance around you in order to bring in more abundance. You draw into your field and environment that which you are drawn to: you attract what you are, not what you think you need or want. Therefore you need to take responsibility for what you attract.

From this space of knowing you can draw balance into your life. There is always a state of flux within the concept of yin and yang, two opposing forces that work independently of one another but cannot be separated. Each one keeps the other in check: if one becomes unbalanced they both become unbalanced. One can be deficient while the other, if left unrestrained, becomes excessive. When you step back and take a look at where there is unbalance within your life you can take measures to create balance once again. You are the creator of your universe, so think carefully about what you want to manifest and take control.

EXERCISE

If you're feeling out of control in a certain area, write down all the experiences you are having. See whether there is a theme occurring and where the negative aspects are. You might want to create a wheel and mark certain aspects of your life on it such as work, exercise, spiritual practices, love and so on. Mark from the centre of the wheel out to each point from 1 to 10, then mark on each scale how much energy you put towards each area in your life. This is usually a good way to see where your focus lies and what areas need more attention.

BEGINNINGS

Lava stone
Beginnings, release, elemental fire
Lava stone, nuumite, obsidian, quartz, scolecite

Lava stones, or scoria, are volcanic rocks that form within lava flows when magma solidifies and hardens. They have tiny bubble holes where gas was forced out when the rocks cooled.

This card indicates a time of great transformation. The crystal grid is made from lava stone, nuumite and obsidian, which are all volcanic rocks or glass created from immense fire elemental energy to create something new, powerful and solid. If force is needed, this is your card. Such deep forces are at play here from the heart of the earth: the fire from within that needs to explode forth and be the creator of something magnificent.

Sometimes having fire or anger inside you can be exactly the energy you need to push through to where you need to be or to achieve something that you didn't think was possible. You will be amazed at what you can achieve with the right impetus. You need to gather all your strength, all your energy or all your fire and direct it into what you desire to manifest or get you through a situation. Allow lava stone to help push you through anything stagnant, which will allow you to release your true potential into something new. If you can imagine it you can create it, and this is the key message here: creation and new beginnings! Yellow and orange within you relate to your ability to create, your fire, creativity and self-esteem.

It's time for you to be a force to be reckoned with, an exciting time that can be like an explosion that will eventually solidify in the present state. Be fluid, allow yourself to release that which no longer serves you and create a fresh beginning for your future or project.

EXERCISE

If you're starting a new project or something is at its beginning stages you might like to carry lava stone with you. There are many pieces of jewellery made from this stone, and you can add essential oils to it; it will absorb the oil so you get the benefits of both the stone and essential oil all day.

A L I G N M E N T

Ilvaite

Alignment, independence, centredness

Ilvaite, onyx, black tourmaline, quartz, citrine

Ilvaite is a relatively rare stone that resembles a very high-quality piece of black tourmaline. It can form in singular columns that look very dense and well terminated. It is a stunning crystal that might show a different colour depending on the light. The message from this stone is one of keeping to yourself. Don't falter in your decision-making or objectives because of the opinions of other people. It's about persevering regardless of what is going on around you. When you're confident in yourself and the wisdom you have obtained over your lifetime you learn to stand your ground, because you are centred and standing in your truth. This means setting strong boundaries, but also when you stand in a place of power your aura becomes impenetrable to lower vibrations. This is strength and a show of independence.

When you are in alignment with who you are, where you're heading and what you stand for no person or thing can shift you off your path. When your purpose is clear you know what to say 'No' to. Does it align with what you believe in? Does it serve your higher self? Will it shift you closer to where you want to be? Ilvaite shows its strength by being an incredibly grounded stone, and we know that all good decision-making comes from a place of being grounded. Remember to stand your ground, but be receptive to higher sources. Nothing can break you or sway you when you're on the path of your highest good. When you're in alignment everything flows.

EXERCISE

Meditate and call in the spirit of ilvaite. Ask for it to share its wisdom with you and sit in its stillness, allowing yourself to feel centred. Feel your strength, feel what it's like to be in true alignment: grounded, peaceful, centred and powerful.

T R U T H

Smithsonite
Truth, open heart, repair

Smithsonite, mangano calcite, quartz, smoky quartz

Smithsonite is mainly recognised for its intense blue colour; however, it does come in other colours as well such as pink, green and brown. It is mainly found as a secondary mineral on a host rock and very rarely forms independent crystals. Being a stone of communication, pink smithsonite allows you to open your heart and speak with love from a place of truth. It is about speaking what is necessary without judgement or damaging words. When you come from a place of love it allows others to receive with love instead of being defensive.

When you speak your truth you allow the energy within you to be released, which can be very healing. It can also be a driving force for the things you are passionate about. Smithsonite tells you it's safe to speak your truth and allows you to push through blocked or stagnant energy, which in turn allows you to release and repair emotional burdens such as feeling unworthy or oppressed. When you align to this truth, this inner empowerment, it raises your vibration so you can break through the patterns or behaviours that may be holding you back. Strength and courage are key.

The truth card is a symbol of power. Are you standing in your truth? We know the saying 'The truth will set you free.' Holding something in that needs to come out can be like stopping water flowing out of a hose by putting a kink in the hose: it's more difficult to hold the water back than it is to let it out. Rather than holding on to negative emotions or something that needs to be said, let it go and allow your body to release the strain of holding it in.

EXERCISE

Is there something you need to say that you have been holding back? If so, call on smithsonite to be with you. You might call it in when you are about to speak your truth or before you write down what you want to say. Get clear and focused on what needs to be said and really look at the words you use: are they inflammatory, and is there a nicer way to get your view across? Are you speaking your truth? Be honest with yourself, because when you speak from this vibration you will be met with the same.

CREATION

Ammonite
Creation, spiralling, growth

Ammonite, tangerine quartz, citrine, quartz, optical calcite

Ammonites are fossilised sea molluscs that became extinct around 65 million years ago. They were creatures with claws and tentacles, and as they grew they added larger chambers to their coil to create the shape seen today. As you grow you need to create larger structures for yourself or you need to expand your views or behaviour. You are not here to play small, and your evolution depends on your growth on all levels.

Growing is about building on what you have already learned or using the knowledge from those before you. Each step is like a building block creating something bigger: each block needs to be put in place before the next one can be laid, and it can't be pushed any quicker than how fast you grow. Everything happens at the right time and at a sustainable pace.

The creation of anything generally starts from a single thought: if you can imagine it, you can create it. This is how your thoughts become things, so you must be clear on what you want to create. Do you need to have a good structured plan and follow it through, or do you need to let the original plan change along the way to allow for the things you learned that you didn't see in the beginning?

Create a structured plan that has breathing room to expand if necessary, as a good plan executed well can bring great success. Allow the creative force to flow through you and your projects and dreams. When you open the gateway to your creativity without putting limits on it, more will come to you. Great things await those who put the work in to making things happen.

EXERCISE

What is it that you want to create? This doesn't always mean something physical: you might wish to create a loving atmosphere in your home, a special place outside or an art piece. Meditate on what you want to create, focusing on how it makes you feel or what you want it to feel like. Allow images or ideas to come to you, then write down or draw images of everything you thought of. Next, decide on your plan of attack: what do you need to do first? Plan out the stages and create a shopping list if you need one, then put it all into action.

JOURNEY

Black calcite

Journeying, lower world, flow

Black calcite, black tourmaline, magnetite, onyx, lava stone, smoky quartz, quartz

Black calcite comes in many shades of colours but is mostly black to grey and sometimes brown, and mostly all with white inclusions. It has a very high carbon content that gives it its black colour. As it is a very dark stone it has beneficial grounding properties, which makes it good for meditating and journeying with. For this reason you might find it under the name of shamanite. I will share the shamanic journey I had with it:

I journeyed to the lower world and called in my spirit animals, one of them being a black panther. She always walks ahead in my journeys to warn me of any dangers. We were underground and there was a path leading to an opening that looked ominous and dark from where I was standing. However, the panther walked along the path and stood outside looking in, waiting for me to catch up. As we entered the cavern our eyes adjusted to the darkness, but when they did there was nothing there: only an empty cavern. I had feared what was in there because I couldn't see what was inside.

The gift in this journey was to recognise that what may seem like a dark tunnel ahead is not to be feared. Fear is a perception of what you envisage something to be, but when you participate and explore you may find that things are not at all what you thought they would be.

There may be many twists and turns or tunnels you have to journey through in life, so be open to the experiences that await you because you don't want to miss something extraordinary while you over-analyse things. Life is a journey, and it's about making the most of the journey to learn and experience as much as you can. It doesn't matter if you don't know what the destination is or what you think it might look like; it's about taking steps forward and pushing through the fears and pre-conceptions you allow to deter you so you can gain a deeper understanding and experience the many wonders waiting in the shadows.

EXERCISE

Is there something you fear that you want to work through? Meditate about the fear you have that is lurking in the cave, or undertake a shamanic journey to the cave to confront it.

See your spirit animals or a protector of some sort walking the path before you, then follow them into the cave and let your eyes become accustomed to the light. See your fear before you, knowing that it cannot harm you in this state. Observe what shape it takes on and ask it what it is trying to teach you. Notice if it changes and be aware of how you feel. Send it love and thank it for the lesson you are being taught. Really take time with this. It might take just one visit for you to understand what the fear is there for, or you can revisit the cave again and again until you feel more comfortable and understand that your fear no longer has a hold on you.

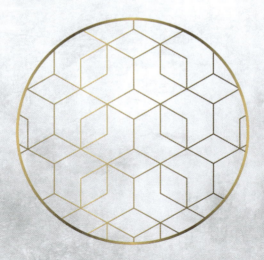

PURPOSE

Eudialyte

Purpose, mission, contracts

Eudialyte, citrine, garnet, quartz, optical calcite

Eudialyte can come in a few different colours but is widely known for its brilliant reddish pink colouring. As it contains the mineral cerium it is classified as mildly radioactive; however, this is not an issue as most of the pieces used in jewellery are small.

Purpose brings up the notion of passion. What are you passionate about: do you have a mission to complete in this lifetime? What gets you up in the morning because you are filled with motivation for it, or do you pry yourself out of bed because you have to go to a job you don't enjoy just to put a roof over your head? This card is asking you whether you are in alignment with your purpose. There doesn't have to be an important quest you must manifest before you die; a purpose can be as small as putting a smile on people's faces when they most need it, or being the parent to a child who will learn their greatest lessons from you.

When you live with purpose you will feel alive and motivated. Do you feel like this? If not, where is your stuck point, or where are you not fulfilling your purpose or desires? Are you feeling constrained by contracts in this lifetime or others? Eudialyte aids with letting you know what direction to take in life as it works strongly with your heart and base chakras. The base chakra represents motivation and your physical strength to do what is needed. If you know what you need to do, make sure you look after your physical body so it can carry you on this journey. Make it sustainable in all ways.

EXERCISE

If you're feeling stuck or lacking purpose it's time to get back to doing what you love and giving yourself space to rest, as sometimes you can search too hard for a label to fit into. Think of something you always wanted to do such as a new hobby or place to visit and put that on your agenda, especially if it's something that keeps coming up time and time again. Follow the intuitive signs and do what makes your heart sing! Even giving yourself the space to relax and just be is enough to allow the messages to come to you more clearly on what your next steps should be. Follow the stepping stones if you don't know where you're meant to end up.

ENDURANCE

Carnelian
Endurance, strength, achievement
Carnelian, garnet, quartz

Carnelian has been prized for centuries and was used as seals and amulets in ancient times. The iron oxide content gives the stone its red colour. It can be fossicked for along rivers or mined underground and will change to a darker colour with heat and sunlight over time. Commercially, it is sometimes treated to make black onyx. How have you endured to make it to where you are now? It may have been a long road, or this card may indicate endurance is needed for the current or future road. Carnelian is a very strong stone that can sit being weathered in the sun for millions of years, and instead of degrading, it changes colour to a vibrant or dark red.

Endurance requires inner strength to weather whatever comes your way. It's about staying true to yourself and either moving forward or remaining where you are, waiting for when it's safe to come out and show yourself. When you endure something you gain a great sense of achievement when it's finished, but do make sure you look after yourself physically, emotionally and spiritually in the process. There is no use standing your ground and creating boundaries that make you hard, so don't lose yourself in the process.

Carnelian has been used for wax seals because hot wax doesn't stick to it. It is also used for protection, and you can understand why when you see how tough it is. Draw on its strength and courage and let everything slide off you. Don't let any negativity get attached.

EXERCISE

If you're feeling worn down from having to endure something that is draining you physically, emotionally or spiritually, carrying carnelian or wearing a necklace made from it can help bring the added protection and endurance you need. Meditating with the stone or this card can bring in the energy of the crystal to help you. When you're drained you can become vulnerable, so calling on external energies to help shield you can provide the extra layer of protection you need at this time.

BRIDGE
Bridge quartz

BRIDGE

Bridge quartz

Bridges, manifestation, breakthrough

Bridge quartz, amethyst, citrine, quartz

Bridge quartz is the name given to the formation of a small crystal that is part inside and part outside another crystal, acting like a bridge between the inside and the outside. The double-terminated quartz crystal in the centre of this grid has a small double-terminated quartz crystal in the lower part, perfectly placed within the main crystal and with just its termination showing outside.

Metaphorically, this card can be asking you to use the energy of a bridge crystal to help you communicate clearer with spirit. Many years ago I was shown by spirit that double-terminated quartz is especially good for two-way communication. This makes sense, as quartz amplifies the energies around it. You can use double-terminated quartz if you don't have a bridge crystal, or just plain quartz will do. With its help you can do channelling work, writing, speaking, art and so on.

Bridges are used to go from one place to another when there is a hurdle in the way. Sometimes you need to look for the bridge or the easier way of crossing a creek, and sometimes you need to build a bridge to get over things. Whatever shape or form the bridge comes in, know that it is you who has to walk over it or build it.

Bridge quartz has similar energies to sceptre quartz. Because the crystal penetrates the other it can help you to get to the root of an issue by really looking deep within. Also, you're working with the energies of two crystals in synchronicity that create a unified field. What can you learn from this? When you work with other people for the same cause you become a stronger force than just you alone, and you can become a bridge for spirit to communicate through you.

EXERCISE

Because there are so many meanings to this card I suggest meditating with bridge quartz and/or amethyst to help you connect with your guides to gain clarity or answers to your questions. You might need to find an easier way of doing things, get past something or overcome a hurdle; either way, elevating your consciousness and tapping into the resources of your guides may provide an easier way for you.

THE KEY

Kammererite
The key, love, knowledge
Kammererite, amethyst, aventurine, quartz

Kammererite is a relatively rare stone that forms a magnificent pinkish-purple crystal. As it is an extremely soft stone it is generally not faceted for use in jewellery. It is mainly found alongside serpentine, which is a beautiful mint-green colour, and the combination of the two is something special. Is there just one key that opens everything, or is life about finding a series of keys to open up the next door for you to step through? When you draw this card it's about finding the key you need to unlock the next chapter: you are the key.

Kammererite has an exceptional way of helping you unlock your soul. Working with the crown, third eye and heart chakras, it allows energy and wisdom to flow through you and unlocks all that clouds you from seeing what you need to and no longer serves you. When you meditate or journey with the energies of this card you can access the infinite wisdom of the universe. It is asking you to travel within in order to find answers from other planes of existence.

Within the centre stone of this grid is a purple heart near the middle. Your heart is the key to unlocking so much more than you know. The universal energy is one of love, so when you resonate at the same vibration and open yourself up to love this energy will come back to you, because you *are* it. Every being on the planet responds to love, whether plant, animal, crystal or human. When you open your heart to love you open your world to receive.

Kammererite allows you to access endless dimensions of knowledge, including the Akashic records. If it is wisdom and guidance you seek, this is your stone. When you unlock the other realms available to you at any time you learn there is no separation and that guidance is just an inner step away.

EXERCISE

If you haven't heard of the Akashic records, it's time to research them. Journeying there can provide you with the information you need to take the next step, as you can access information from all lifetimes past, present and future. It is like a library, and once you journey there you will understand how much benefit it can be. Meditating with this stone and simply asking for it to share its knowledge with you while you sit with it will be highly beneficial. Take notice of any signs you receive, whether they are visual, words, feelings, smells or any other way you receive your signs, and remember that spirit communicates with us in many ways.

FOUNDATIONS

Pyrite

Foundations, structure, grounding

Pyrite, citrine over morion, smoky quartz, quartz, pyrite

Pyrite, or fool's gold, has a brass-yellow, metallic lustre and forms in many interesting structures, including beautiful cubes and octahedrons. When you create anything you want to last you must ensure you lay strong foundations. If you fail to do so by rushing or not being thorough, it won't matter how good the structure on top is: it will have weaknesses. Understand the importance of what you start today and make sure you don't take short cuts. Dot all the i's and cross all the t's. This card may be confirmation that you have laid good foundations for what's ahead.

Pyrite can contain gold within it and can also create a spark when struck against metal or stone, embracing the fire element and the spark of new ideas, wealth and power. It brings inner strength as well as offering protection from external sources. It is a powerful card to pull and a positive stone that is often overlooked and seldom recognised for its amazing benefits. Is it really fool's gold, then? Don't be quick to judge if there isn't a monetary value to something, as the true benefits may be something quite unique.

Pyrite is an excellent stone for manifestation, as it helps with mental stability, memory and willpower as well as promoting positive thinking and confidence. Your base chakra is also the foundation for the other chakras, which means that you must look after your physical body so you can achieve your goals. Ensure you are well grounded when you make any decisions.

EXERCISE

If you feel as though your foundations are not stable, it may be time to find a way to strengthen them. Do you need to revisit your plans, come up with a strategy or find new ways of doing things? Look after your physical self with nourishing foods and exercise, and make your relationships stronger by giving them more of your attention and time. Whatever it is, find the weak spots and decide on a plan to make them stronger.

GRATITUDE

Grossularite
Gratitude, regeneration, optimism
Grossularite, citrine, onyx, quartz

Grossularite is green garnet, which means that it also holds the same properties as red garnet. It comes in many colours except for blue and is an important stone for recognising that abundance is all around you. When you show your gratitude for something you in turn feel abundance, and when you feel both abundance and gratitude together you draw more of the same. Gratitude is an extremely high vibration that resonates like love does, and the higher you raise your vibration the more you will draw these higher energies to you. Gratitude is so important in your life and for allowing manifestation to occur. What are you grateful for in your life at present? How can you bring more gratitude and abundance into it? If you wish to manifest something in your life, you need to sit in the feeling as though it has already happened, because you manifest what you are and not what you need. If you wish to create abundance, you must feel abundance in your life.

Grossularite is known as a regenerative stone, as well as being one of prosperity. It can help release limitations you have physically and emotionally or to do with your health or wealth. It allows you to relax and go with the flow, which allows your body to heal itself. Because it holds the same qualities as normal garnet it helps create stability, confidence and motivation to make things happen.

EXERCISE

Meditate or journey and imagine you are doing something you wish to manifest or achieve. Visualise sitting in the future moment as though it is the present, and feel the vibration of gratitude flowing through you. Thank the energies that have helped make it happen and bask in the beautiful feeling of achievement, then let it go and know that it is on its way.

SOUL STAR

Apophyllite
Soul star, truth, uplifting
Apophyllite, amethyst, quartz, optical calcite

Apophyllite forms in stunning pyramid-like formations as well as cubes and druzy over matrix. It can come in many colours, the green being particularly beautiful, but it is normally seen in a clear colour. This is a high vibrational card as apophyllite helps you to attune to higher dimensions and realms. If you connect your third eye and crown chakras with the help of apophyllite you will be able to understand the information you gain from above.

This is a time to meditate more in order to find the answers you seek. Looking for guidance from above and from where your soul resides is necessary when the answers are not clear. Pay attention to your dreams and keep a piece of apophyllite or this card next to your bed. You can both meditate and shamanic journey with apophyllite; some people like to place the crystals on their eyes or third eye when they do so.

Remember that when you access higher planes of reality you must always remain grounded. You may receive information, but if you aren't grounded you may not fully understand what you are receiving or being presented. Pairing apophyllite with black tourmaline is a beautiful combination, or you can meditate outside with your feet touching the earth. The more you create a union between the higher and lower realms the more balanced you will feel when you create this connection. When you create a higher connection you will be uplifted and energised and able to discern truth. Connect with your higher truth and don't let denser reality pull you down. Now is the time to rise above.

EXERCISE

Meditate with a piece of apophyllite on your eye or third eye or place this card next to you. Alternatively, you can simply ask the energy of apophyllite to be with you. You don't need a specific question to ask when doing this, just enjoy blissing out and relaxing and see what comes to you. It might be images, feelings, words or smells. Allow yourself to just let go and see where it takes you.

CALM

Green opal

Calm, cleansing, heartache

Green opal, orange kyanite, quartz, optical calcite

Green opal is a very common form of opal. The beautiful green hue comes from the inclusion of the mineral nontronite. A period of calm is needed or is coming your way. Whether you are overcoming some sort of heartache or loss or maybe just stuck in a thought pattern that's creating stress, it's time for you to calm your heart by cleansing yourself of these emotions. This is a great card to pull when you are going through a transitional phase, as it indicates that it too shall pass and that once you let go of the energy that is causing you pain you allow new, loving thoughts and feelings to come your way.

When green opal is coupled with orange kyanite, which is known to be a powerful emotional cleanser, you can make a very fast shift. The slower and calmer you become the better the space you give yourself to feel what you need to so you can then let it go. Once you do this work you no longer have to keep replaying and revisiting the experience because you have dealt with it. Green opal helps join the heart and mind together and orange kyanite works with your emotions and creativity, so perhaps it's time to think or be creative and allow the flow to happen naturally. Green opal is known as the feel-good stone. Be calm, cleanse and open your heart again. Let go and move on.

This card asks you to not lay blame, but to observe your own behaviours and see what you can leave behind. This may be how you treat others or how you treat yourself.

EXERCISE

If you need to find calm, obtain a piece of green opal or use this card to meditate with. When you can no longer control the environment around you it's time to change the environment within you. Do whatever you need to do to find your piece of calm. Go for a gentle walk, sit on the beach, read a book in your PJs or have a cup of your favourite tea with your cat sitting beside you. It can be anything you enjoy, but it needs to bring you calm. Your body needs calm to heal and replenish itself, and only you can make this happen.

INNER DIVINITY

Garnierite

Inner divinity, self-worth, unconditional love

Garnierite, peridot, quartz, optical calcite

Garnierite, which is also known as green moonstone, is a member of the feldspar family. Its characteristic mint-green colour is due to the presence of nickel and it is known for its connection with emotions, so the presence of green within the stone indicates it can heal the emotions of your heart. It helps with loving yourself and recognising your inner divinity, because when you understand how special you are you no longer need to search out gratification from external sources.

When you love who you are inside and out you radiate a positivity that is infectious to everyone around you. You cannot help but lift others. You don't need to be perfect to realise your inner divinity, for there is no such thing as perfection. Accepting yourself for all of your parts, behaviours and past experiences is key to understanding you are here to learn, have fun and love other people.

The calming colour and qualities of garnierite are good for calming stress and anxiety, so when you're feeling particularly emotional you need to do whatever it takes to calm yourself. Living with stress and anxiety is never good for you body so you must learn what these emotions are telling you, and garnierite can help with this. It can also help manage anger and bring you back to a place of unconditional love, a place from which you are able to view people and situations differently and without judgement. You can then make better decisions, as they will not be affected by unstable emotions.

EXERCISE

If you're finding it difficult to see your inner divinity and beauty it is time to sit with this card. You don't need to try to analyse what you feel is good or bad about yourself; just sit and be. Allow yourself to be showered with love, and if you feel emotional and need to cry then do so. Let it out. Ask for the gifts of garnierite to be with you and help show you how beautiful you are, even if you are unable to see it. Be kind to yourself.

LUCIDITY

Mtorolite

Lucidity, weather the storm, nurture

Mtorolite, epidote, selenite, aventurine, quartz, optical calcite

Mtorolite is also known as chrome chalcedony and is commonly found in Zimbabwe. It is a cryptocrystalline variety of quartz, meaning that it is an aggregate of many smaller crystals.

This card represents the need to be lucid or fluid while weathering a storm, and it can provide the strength and endurance you need to ride it out. Storms don't last forever; they eventually pass, and all you need to do is take cover and wait it out. It is out of your control, so you don't need to worry yourself about what the outcome will be because you can cross that bridge when you come to it. What you can do is remain calm and surrender to the beautiful energy that is cleansing your surroundings and will eventually bring sunshine.

Mtorolite helps you to connect with your heart chakra, ultimately where you find balance between your internal and external environments. It is the centre of your chakra system, and when there is imbalance there it creates a disharmony between the upper and lower chakras. Balancing this area can give us the ability to work from a place of love, giving and receiving.

Folklore suggests mtorolite supports the practice of working with plant medicines of all types. Connecting with the plant realm requires connection through your heart. You can endure, you can find strength and you will heal and cope with whatever life throws at you. Remember that everything that happens *to* you is *for* you, so what can you learn from your experiences? How can you make the most of what you have been dealt, or how can you rise above what might seem unsurmountable? While you're weathering the storm somewhere safe and calm, take some time to ponder these questions.

EXERCISE

Is there an area in your life that would benefit from you being more fluid? Are you weathering the storm or do you feel as though you are in the midst of it? Meditate with this card or journey to meet the spirit of the stone, and ask the stone or your guides to help you find fluidity in your situation. Where is it safe to wait out the storm? Perhaps you are creating the storm or drawing the storm to you. Look inside for your answers.

SUCCESS

Myrickite

Success, power, vitality

Myrickite, Herkimer diamond, quartz, optical calcite

Myrickite is also known as opalised or agatised cinnabar and the merchant's stone. The stone in the centre of the grid is agatised. The opalised version comes in black with red-orange colouring.

Myrickite is said to remove obstacles and attract prosperity. As well as attracting wealth, it helps maintain a state of wealth. Success may be on its way or is already here: what does success look like for you? Success means different things to different people, so this card may be asking you what exactly it is that you want. This card represents vitality and power, two qualities that aid in achieving success. Are you standing in your power or are you allowing it to be drained in areas that won't bring you success? Are you letting others draw from you because you haven't set strong enough boundaries? Are you looking after yourself physically so that when success comes you can sustainably manage it? Is what you're doing in order to gain success bringing you joy?

When you gain success you usually feel excited, proud and happy. If you're not feeling those things you need to reassess and really dig down into your core to see what you truly want, even if you think it's not achievable. Anything is possible if you believe it is. Stay true to yourself and others, because success is not success if you hurt those around you in the process. Find inner strength and aim for what you want, because it will be yours.

EXERCISE

Have you really sat down and thought out what success actually looks like for you? Perhaps it's time to write it down. You can't manifest success if you don't know what it looks like for you. It might be as simple as being in a happy, loving relationship with a partner or living in a home you love or it can be more elaborate, such as working for yourself in a business you love or publishing a book. When you know where you want to be, the universe will make way for you. Once you know where you want to be you can make a plan and take action on how to get there. Call in the spirit of the myrickite to be with you and help you while you think it out.

NATURE SPIRIT

Chlorite in quartz
Nature spirit, growth, cleansing
Chlorite in quartz, epidote, aegirine, pyrite, quartz

Chlorite is a member of the mica group and is widely found within many types of metamorphic rocks, which means they have started out in one form only to be changed to another form under certain conditions such as heat or pressure. It's what gives the quartz centrepiece in the grid its distinctive deep emerald green colour.

In order to grow you must lay down strong roots that you can draw from. Chlorite in quartz helps you connect with the realm of nature spirits and fae as well as resonate with the soul of the earth. For this reason it is also a strong cleanser that aids in self-healing and regeneration of your body. Coupled with the striking piece of aegirine above it, chlorite in quartz makes a high vibrational card of cleansing and aligning yourself to nature.

The fae and nature spirits are not like the romanticised artworks of the Victorian era; they are energy beings that have been here for millennia and sometimes choose to work with humankind. Creating a strong connection with them requires respect and an open heart. Be aware of the green of the stones, the green of nature and the green of your heart chakra: all are connected, and all can help heal on physical, emotional and spiritual levels.

When you allow yourself to become aligned with nature you allow nature to cleanse you, and you become an open channel to your natural surroundings. When you cleanse you make room for fresh energy to come into your being, and this helps you to grow. Working with nature and your heart centre is vital for your body and spirit. Allow the fae and nature spirits to guide you.

Do you feel drawn to working with plants or herbs, even something as simple as wanting to get a pot plant? This could be your calling to start exploring or expanding on this area.

EXERCISE

This is good exercise to do outside where you can sit on the ground, under a tree or close to a pot plant. If you don't have chlorite in quartz you can use quartz or a dark green stone, or sit with this card and call in the spirit of the chlorite quartz. Close your eyes and focus on breathing deeply in and out.

Imagine when you are breathing in that you are breathing straight into your heart centre, and then breathe out through your nose or mouth. Feel yourself breathing love into your heart and then breathe love out to whatever is in front of you: plant or tree or park. Establish a strong cycle of breathing in love and breathing out love until you can feel the plant respond and the love expanding. Do this for as long as you like and repeat as many times as needed.

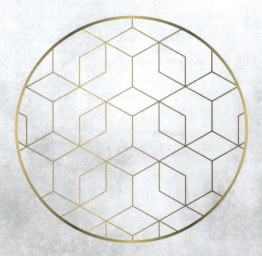

IMPACT

Campo del Cielo

Impact, clearing the path, speed

Campo del Cielo, quartz, black obsidian, onyx, optical calcite

Campo del Cielo was a group of meteorites that landed in Argentina close to 5,000 years ago. The area they landed in was most likely named after this occurrence, as it translates to 'field of the sky or heaven'. It is composed mostly of iron and nickel. Meteorites are very potent pieces that are sacred to many cultures worldwide. They fly at great speed through space, colliding with objects along the way, and the impact they create when they hit earth is immense.

Meteorite energy, one of high vibration but also dense grounding, helps align all your chakras and strengthens your aura. It may be time to completely break down your idea of yourself. Whatever it is, something will have a big impact on you or you will make a big impact in some way. Because Campo del Cielo is very protective, it can safeguard you against impacts from external sources, both emotional and spiritual.

Know that when this card appears in a reading it means something big, something that hits with such force it leaves a trace and ripples outwards. Everything that comes your way is a positive no matter how it first appears, so you should be grateful for lessons that are given from external forces. This is a time to be completely focused on what you want and where you are headed. Go straight for what you want and do not detour, because the speed with which you direct your energy into something will have a lasting impact.

EXERCISE

Is there an area of your life in which you need to clear a path? You might not know how to but there are ways you can use meditation to help you achieve your goal. You need to know what it looks like on the other side of your obstacle, and when you can visualise that you need to sit in the feeling as though it has already happened even if you're unsure of how you will get there. Feeling gratitude and joy while you are meditating will allow you to attract that scenario to you, instead of the one you are in now. The universe will guide you through. Sometimes the greatest changes can come completely from out of nowhere.

BIGGER PICTURE
Wavellite

BIGGER PICTURE

Wavellite
Bigger picture, clearing the way, compassion
Wavellite, quartz, aventurine

Wavellite, a phosphate mineral that forms clusters, comes in beautiful shades of green, from emerald, pale and bright to apple green.

It's time to look at the bigger picture. There may be something you need to look at from a different point of view and change your dialogue about. Do you want something better for yourself but can't work out why it's not manifesting? You might be looking at it from the wrong angle. For instance, you might want to leave your job so you can follow your passion and your question keeps returning to: 'When am I going to leave?' Instead, say to yourself: 'I look forward to living my passion of helping others.' Feel the difference in energy or emotion that comes from both of these statements, one coming from a place of hopelessness, desperation and negativity and one from positivity, optimism and joy. When you change the dialogue you keep repeating you also change the emotion of the statements.

Sometimes you can't see the forest for the trees. Take a deep breath, step back and focus on what is in front of you. Answers are not always black and white, and sometimes the truth is something you don't see. Ask what the bigger picture is, what you are not seeing and how you can learn from this. Remember that we are here to learn lessons and grow and we are not perfect. You are human, and when you step back to see the bigger picture you can see things with more compassion and love.

EXERCISE

If there is a situation you need to see from a different angle then journeying or mediating with wavellite could be very beneficial. Set the intention of the journey or meditation as being able to see the bigger picture, and ask for spirit to guide you to see from a different angle what you're not seeing in this moment. You could also ask for spirit to show you in your dreams or send you a sign. Calling in eagle or owl medicine is also good for this work, as they soar high above and see with such precision. Owls can see well in the dark and seek out truth, so if something is hidden then owl will help you find it.

BREAKTHROUGH
Azurite

BREAKTHROUGH

Azurite

Breakthrough, detox, speaking up

Azurite, quartz, lapis lazuli

Azurite has a distinctive blue colour due to its high copper content. As it is a very soft mineral it is not commonly used in jewellery. It is often found with malachite, another copper-containing mineral. A breakthrough is imminent if it has not already arrived. This is an extremely positive card as azurite helps you push through and overcome obstacles, something that might have been blocking you for some time or that you needed to get off your chest. As it is a beautiful blue colour this card also resonates with your throat chakra, the chakra of communication and expression. Is there something you need to say or do you need to express yourself more wholly? It may indicate a breakthrough in your thinking, behaviours or even a project or relationship.

It's time to remove all the blockages in your life so you can create a healthy flow, because wherever there is a block there is an excess building up behind it. This excess needs to be allowed to flow freely, and azurite is a good stone for detoxing. You can detox in many ways, such as physically clearing out your physical surroundings, removing people from your life or getting rid of bad habits. Either way, when you remove the blockages you leave room for fresh things to flow into that space.

It could be time to speak up for yourself and shake off any guilt, anger or people pleasing. Push aside all that no longer serves you and face your fears; you might find that it's not as hard as you imagine it to be. Push forward and through what stands in your way.

EXERCISE

If you're feeling stuck in any area of your life or you need to get something off your chest, meditating with azurite could help. When you begin your meditation, call in your guides and the spirit of azurite and ask it to share its knowledge and help you make the breakthrough you need. The answers may not come straight away, but pay attention to the signs you notice or the 'A-ha' moments. These are the signposts that will guide you through.

FLOW

Caribbean calcite
Flow, calmness, allowing

Caribbean calcite, hemimorphite, quartz, Herkimer diamond, optical calcite

Caribbean calcite is a relatively new find that contains blue calcite along with brown and white aragonite, which makes it a particularly striking stone. This card indicates a time to just be, to let go and allow yourself to be free of judgement, restrictions, limitations or stress. Allow flow to occur and take away your stresses, tensions and fears. All is what it is meant to be.

When you let go and allow the flow to take you where you are meant to go instead of pushing yourself where you think you should be going you allow a higher energy to step in and guide you. This higher presence can see the path before you that you don't see. Allow this presence into your life and watch as magnificent things unfold. Things become easier when we flow with them instead of pushing them. Get in tune with the pace the flow needs to be, and if you feel like you're swimming upstream against the current remember that you can swim sideways, which will bring you to the bank.

Learning and feeling the currents of ebbs and flows within your body and your surroundings can be helpful on so many levels. Learn when you need to rest and when you can harness your energy to achieve big goals. When it all feels too hard, know that that is the time you need to sit back, rest and let it flow to you. It is in the moments of downtime that you gain much clarity and knowledge, because it is only when you calm your mind and body that spirit can clearly communicate with you. Spirit's message is clear: remain calm and grounded and you will find your flow.

EXERCISE

If you are pushing things too hard or exhausting yourself and getting nowhere, it's an indication that you may not be in flow. This card tells you to take your hands off the steering wheel and take time out. Slow down, grab a cuppa and sit outside and just be; getting in the flow can be as simple as that. Meditating with Caribbean calcite can also assist. Feel the calm energies like the gentle swell of the sea, and allow the water energy of the crystal to help you find your flow again. Visit the sea or any place of water or call in the water elementals with a water fountain. Allow yourself to relax and let what needs to come to you flow gently.

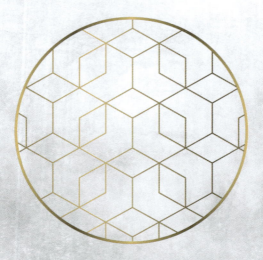

OPTIMISM

Cavansite

Optimism, joy, transition

Cavansite, quartz

Cavansite is a rare, small stone usually found as little rosettes on a bed of other minerals. Its characteristic bright blue colour is the only colour in which it is found. It's a powerful stone that will help you through major changes in your life, as it helps you transition and find optimism along the way. The future is bright! This card is here to give you the courage and confidence to know that where you're headed is exactly where you're meant to be. You are an amazing manifestor, so know that what you are going through is because you are destined for something better. This transition will pass, so maintain your optimism and face it with joy.

A stone of truth and expression, cavansite will help you see through doubts and pressures as well as help you connect with your guides and intuition so you can see what needs to be seen. For this reason it is a very useful stone to use in meditation. Cavansite allows you to follow your innermost truths with joy and optimism and will create an abundance of joy and optimism in your life. When you follow your truth with joy and optimism you are in a state of flow, which is an indication that you are on your spiritual path. From this state, more things to be joyful and optimistic about will be drawn to you. Everything will turn out for the best, but whatever the outcome is, it is for your highest good.

EXERCISE

Is there something you wish for or something you need to be optimistic about? This card is about joy and transition. If you cannot sense optimism, be gentle with yourself as you go through the transition and call on cavansite to help you be optimistic. Even if what you hoped for doesn't come, know that something awaits you at the end that you might not be able to see right now.

EXPANSION

Brookite

Expansion, ascension, motivation

Brookite, Herkimer diamond, quartz

Brookite is normally found in black, brown, reddish brown and occasionally white. It is fairly rare compared with other crystals and is generally only found as quite small specimens. It is a high vibrational stone regardless of its size, a stone of expansion in every facet of your life: the expansion of your ideas, spirituality and thinking, which are growing in every way for the better. You have done the work of clearing, because in order to expand you must make room to grow just as a spider or snake sheds its skin to allow it to grow bigger. It is still the same in many ways on the outside, but small spurts of growth over time add up to large changes overall.

Brookite holds immense energy, so if you're seeking enlightenment and motivation for your spiritual purpose then this is your stone. Any stone that holds a high vibration holds positivity, because negativity is a lower vibration. Remember this when you need to be uplifted. Surround yourself with higher vibrational people and objects, which can only lead to you being lifted up. There are endless possibilities awaiting you and many doors to walk through, no matter what direction you take. The more open you are to the limitless possibilities available to you the less you will hold yourself back.

Brookite is known for its ability to help make and maintain contact with higher beings waiting to assist you. Know that all your questions can be answered by asking, so rise above and expand your awareness.

EXERCISE

This is a feel-good stone that will allow you to expand into the infinite being you are. You can meditate with brookite by setting your intent on finding answers to the questions you have, or journey with it to make contact with higher beings purely with the intent of learning from them and asking what wisdom they would like to impart to you.

BLOOM

Cerasite
Blooming, transition, motivation
Cerasite, golden Herkimer diamond, rose quartz, quartz

Cerasite, or cherry blossom stone, is a very unique stone from Japan. It starts off as a mineral called cordierite, but when it is naturally hydrothermally altered, it turns into mica and becomes cerasite. What makes it special is that it looks like the cherry blossoms of Japan. These stones are tiny; the centrepiece of this grid is just four millimetres wide.

You don't need to be big to blossom. You have undergone massive changes that can only happen under the right circumstances and have come through the other side stronger and shining a radiance that is seldom seen. Just like the beauty of the cherry blossom, when we bloom we all bloom together; we are beautiful, breathtaking even. Something draws us in that we can't stop looking at, and while each cherry blossom is beautiful on its own, when seen as a whole in the different stages of growth it is something to behold.

The bloom indicates all the work you have put in to change who you are as a spiritual, emotional and physical being. It may have been a time of great pressure or emotion, but the stress has paid off. You are now through and ready to show the world what you have to offer.

Like cherry blossoms, cerasite is incredibly delicate and can be crushed between your fingers; the Japanese sometimes coat them to preserve their beauty. A single flower only gets the chance to bloom once, but every time you go through a transition you can bloom again and again, especially when you know how it worked out for you last time. You might welcome upheaval and transition when you understand that things will work out for the best.

EXERCISE

It is time to bloom: dress in your favourite clothes, wear your favourite jewellery, go to your favourite places and shine your glow from the inside. Stand tall and be proud of who you have become and spread that vibration everywhere you go, just like the petals of the cherry blossom tree floating on the wind. Your energy is beautiful in this state and will affect all who come into your presence for the positive.

AMPLIFY

Rhodizite
Amplification, strength, influence
Rhodizite, Herkimer diamond, quartz

Rhodizite are tiny crystals that average around four millimetres in length. They are relatively colourless crystals that can be white or yellow. Although the crystals are small in size they are powerful amplifiers, especially when used in combination with other stones. This is why they are sometimes known as master crystals. They don't need to be cleansed or charged. What thoughts are you putting out at the moment, and is this something you want amplified?

If it is positive then, yes, let it be amplified, but if you're putting out negative thoughts and ideas it's time to focus on what you want to achieve and become the manifestor of your dreams.

Rhodizite is an excellent crystal that will aid meditation because of its interaction with your higher chakras. It helps you enhance the gifts you already have and assists with communication with higher realms. It reminds you of your personal power: no matter how small you think you are you can have an impact on the world by being like a ripple in a pond. Rhodizite also works with your solar plexus chakra, which allows you to find your confidence and personal power. It helps you understand the lessons you have learned to get to this point and how you can use them to aid you in this lifetime. What you send out to the world is amplified, so be sure to align with and fully know in your heart what you wish to put your energy into.

EXERCISE

Think about something you really want to bring into your life or make happen; this could be as simple as wanting a calm atmosphere to live in to a big project you want to get off the ground. Write down in detail in the present tense what it feels like to have it already, then call on the spirit of rhodizite to be with you to show you how to amplify the right message to call in your wish. Remain in the feeling of it already being there and allow all the positive feelings to well up inside you: gratitude, love, joy and peace. Remain in this present moment of achieving your desires and expressing the emotions as long as you can, then picture yourself sending out this vibration all around the earth. You will be surprised by how powerful this can be!

STRENGTH

Diamond
Strength, shining, influence
Diamond, rose quartz, quartz

Diamonds are created under extreme temperature and pressure. As the exact conditions needed to form diamonds have not occurred in our lifetime, the age when they were created was millions of years ago. They are not made from coal as first thought, but from carbon.

Diamonds have forever been seen as the gift of long-lasting love, as they are virtually unbreakable. They are incredibly hard and strong and are thus used to cut all other gemstones. They are a symbol of strength and endurance, and because of their stunning refractive qualities when cut, they also allow you to shine through adversity. Shine in the glory of knowing how strong you have become or how strong you need to be at this time. Strength can come from many sources; it can be gained from wisdom through dealing with pressure and adversity over your lifetime or from having family and friends in your corner when you need them. Strength comes from following what makes your heart sing, so find what brings your greatest strength from within and use it to your advantage. No one can stand in your way when you lead with internal power.

The radiance from a beautifully cut diamond is something to behold: the way the light refracts perfectly, pulling your gaze to its magnificence. Beauty is in the eye of the beholder, and you are beautiful because of what you have gone through, just as diamonds did in their formation. Some people love diamonds with flaws, as they view the flaws as adding to a diamond's lustre. Other people prefer absolute perfection, but this mainly indicates a true reflection of the person who is looking at the diamond. You often look for that which is similar to yourself, so understand that if you're seeking perfection you may be striving for perfection within yourself to start with. However, if you seek diamonds with flaws you can relate, because you love your flaws as they make you you.

EXERCISE

Take some time to record what you think your strengths and weaknesses are. Look at what you perceive to be your flaws: how can you turn them into strengths, or where can you use your strengths to get you where you need to be? If you know what your strengths and weaknesses are you can change course or tactics in situations or you can strengthen the areas that need some work. This allows you to become multifaceted in many areas.

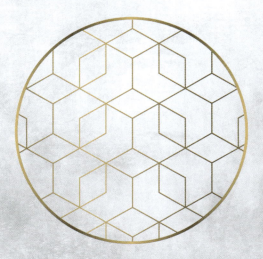

INTUITION

You
Intuition, strength, influence
Quartz

Quartz, the most abundant mineral on earth, is known as the master healer and for good reason. It amplifies everything it comes into contact with, so just having it in your presence is enough to raise your vibration. This card has a basic grid that needs something added to it in order to complete it. It is indicating that it may be time to ask yourself what you need. What is your intuition telling you? How can you look inside instead of looking externally for your answers? It's time to take matters into your own hands and make an intuitive decision. We use our brain and logic to make decisions, so when we hit a dead end it's time to turn to our intuition. Sometimes the answers will not be black and white but will be many shades of grey. You could go around for days or months trying to work it out, but when it comes down to it you have to go with your gut. It is never wrong.

You might have a strong feeling about someone or something but are not confident you're reading things right. Always trust your gut instincts, as they are there to warn you as well as guide you. When you allow yourself to be guided by your intuition you allow other possibilities to come to you that you may not have thought of. This guidance comes from a higher source, from your guides and your soul. This is the place you should always go when it is answers that you seek. Let *you* be your guide.

EXERCISE

Try to intuitively make your own grid. You can place whatever you like on this card or you can make one yourself. Be drawn by the colours, crystals or plants that feel right to you. Is there a theme? Do they relate to any specific chakra? How does it make you feel? What are the words, smells, feelings or thoughts that come to you? It's up to you to follow your intuition because it is always right.

ABOUT THE AUTHOR AND ILLUSTRATOR

Nicola McIntosh is the artist and author of the *Crystal Grid Oracle* and *Crystal Grid Secrets*. As she has worked with crystals for close to 30 years, including gem cutting, she has created a strong relationship with them and their uses. She has a background in Western and Chinese herbal medicine as well as Celtic shamanism, and has brought her wealth of knowledge together to create tools to help people take ownership of their own healing on a spiritual and emotional level. She has also released the book *Plant Spirit Medicine* and another oracle deck, *Celtic Spirit Oracle*.

When we do the inner work the outer changes, and this is Nicola's wish for all. We are all here to learn and grow, but most of all to help each other. You can find Nicola here:

www.spiritstone.com.au

 spirit.stone

 SpiritStoneCrystals

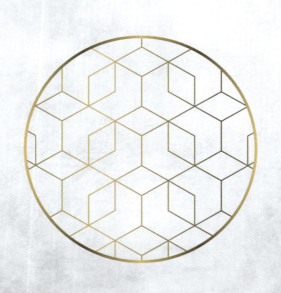